Finding the End of the Rainbow

A STORY OF HOPE, CHANGE, FORGIVENESS, AND REDEMPTION

VICKY BERRY

FINDING THE END OF THE RAINBOW
A Story of Hope, Change, Forgiveness, and Redemption
Vicky Berry

To contact the author, email: vickyb2@comcast.net
www.findingtheendoftherainbow.com

Published by:

Mary Ethel

Mary Ethel Eckard
Frisco, Texas

Library of Congress Control Number: 2023921942
ISBN (Print): 979-8-9894822-0-7
ISBN (eBook): 979-8-9894822-1-4

Unless otherwise noted, all Scripture is taken from THE HOLY BIBLE, NEW INTERNATIONAL VERSION® NIV® Copyright © 1973, 1978, 1984 by International Bible Society. ® Used by permission.

DEDICATION

This book is dedicated to the precious Lord.
Not only did He save me
but He also taught me about His unconditional forgiveness.
By allowing Him to place His forgiveness in my heart,
I fly with Him above the clouds,
over the rainbow
every day
and I live redeemed, forgiven, and free.

CONTENTS

SECTION III
GOD'S RAINBOW APPEARS

INTRODUCTION

We all experience difficult times. Many of us immerse ourselves in music to help soothe those rough spots. Sometimes it works, other times it doesn't.

In my lifetime, rainbows have always symbolized change, forgiveness, redemption, and hope that a new day would begin; a day without pain. Judy Garland's 1939 signature song, "Somewhere Over the Rainbow," was my go-to song that helped me cope during tough moments. I can't begin to count how many times I looked out my bedroom window in hopes that a rainbow would appear. My desperation to end the hardship I experienced was fierce.

During my pregnancy at the age of seventeen, which was one of the roughest seasons of my life, I sang this song daily. Even after my child was born and abruptly taken away, I kept singing it, as it brought comfort and a belief that someday my child and I would be reunited. I believed what the Lord promised in Genesis 9:13-16.

"I will remember my covenant between me and you and all living creatures of every kind. Never again will the waters become a flood to destroy all life. Whenever the rainbow appears in the clouds, I will see it and remember the everlasting covenant between God and all living creatures of every kind on the earth."

I had faith that the Lord would help me through everything if I fully trusted in Him. Jesus said, "*Truly I tell you, if you have faith like a grain of mustard seed, you can say to this mountain, 'Move from here to there,' and it will move. Nothing will be impossible for you.*" Matthew 17:20

The Lord continually confirmed His promise and His presence to me through the rainbow. I am not exaggerating when I say that I saw Him at the end of each rainbow when the sun appeared, marking the end of a tribulation period in my life. He kept hope alive in my heart.

One day as I was jogging and listening to the song, "You and I" by Celine Dion, it felt like something hit me head-on and I stopped in my tracks. The lyrics were:

You and I were meant fly

Higher than the clouds we'll sail across the sky

So come with me and you will feel

That we're soaring, that we're floating up so high

Cause you and I were meant to fly.[1]

I knew I was in the Lord's presence. I had a vision of the two of us flying over the rainbow above the clouds. He said that I had forgiven so many people all my life, but I still had anger in my heart because I could not **forget** and deal with the hurt, which meant I was not forgiving unconditionally. I realized that, rather than dealing with the anger and pain, I had placed them in a box and thrown away the key. I had failed to understand that, before I could move from a difficult situation, I had to forgive those who caused me the pain, shame, and hopelessness that led to the tribulation. These hurts were not easy to forgive, and the anger was not easy to release, even with the Lord's help. I had lived under the assumption that I could try to forgive and move on, but the Lord told me that

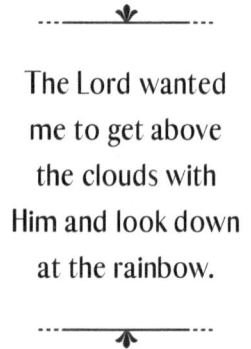

The Lord wanted me to get above the clouds with Him and look down at the rainbow.

was not the case. He showed me that, to truly move on, I must fully surrender my heart to Him and He would give me His unconditional forgiveness, both for myself and for those who hurt me. He said that forgiveness must be given in His way and not mine, and that His unconditional forgiveness was the only way to **true freedom** from the anger, shame, and hurt I carried.

Isn't that true in our lives as Christians? We forgive because it is what the Lord asks us to do, but we do not forget. It is the typical attitude, "I forgive you, but I will never forget," which leads to anger and anxiety in our hearts. Instead of forgetting, we bury the emotions and pain and carry them with us.

The Lord did not just want me to get beyond the promise at the end of the rainbow. He wanted me to get above the clouds with Him and look down at the rainbow. The power of His unconditional forgiveness for and through me allowed me to unconditionally forgive others. How could He be telling me, after all my many traumas, that through Him I could unconditionally forgive and be redeemed?

This experience was miraculous, life-changing, and redemptive. His forgiveness is available for all who are open to receive His truth and walk in His ways. Open your heart to our Lord and His bigger plan for your life and to the unconditional forgiveness He has for you and for those who have hurt you. The Lord's forgiveness helped me remove the heavy emotional anvil of unforgiveness so I can soar high above the rainbow with Him. I pray the same blessing for you!

> *"Bear with each other and forgive one another if any of you have a grievance against someone. Forgive as the Lord forgave you."*
> Colossians 3:13

SECTION I

A Storm is Brewing

"Who is wise? He will realize these things,
Who is discerning? He will understand them.
The ways of the Lord are right;
The righteous walk in them,
But the rebellious stumble in them."

—Hosea 14:9

CHAPTER 1

In the Beginning

The 1930s were dark and troubling times with the Great Depression, factory shutdowns, foreclosures on farms and homes, unemployment, hunger, poverty, and abandoned mines and mills. The 1940s brought World War II, the Holocaust, atomic bombs, and the beginning of the Cold War.

The 1950s was a time of booming economy and is generally portrayed favorably through television shows like *Happy Days, Leave it to Beaver,* and *Father knows Best.* People were ready to let loose and have fun. Music changed with incredible singers and many bands emerged that appealed to all tastes. The birth of rock and roll came onto the scene with Elvis Pressley leading the way. Black and white televisions adorned the living rooms of most American households debuting *The Mickey Mouse Club* and the first episode of *Gunsmoke.* The first MacDonald's was built, and Disneyland in Anaheim, California opened. In that decade, Americans could optimistically pursue what was coined the American Dream, which included the comforts of home ownership, material possessions that were previously difficult to attain (or simply not invented yet), and good times.

Historians use the word *boom* to describe many things about the 1950s: the booming economy, the booming suburbs, and, of course, the baby boom. This boom began in 1946 when a record number of babies (3.4 million) were born in the United States. In the 1950s, about four million babies were born each year. By the time the boom finally tapered off in 1964, there were almost seventy-seven million baby boomers.

1955 was also the year the average suburban house price was a mere $2,064, yet the average car price was $1,900. Eighteen cents would buy a loaf of bread, ninety-two cents would buy a gallon of milk, and the cost for a gallon of gas was twenty-three cents. This sounds good, but the minimum hourly pay rate was $1. Many families could survive on one income, many others could not. 1955 was also the year the Vietnam conflict started.

I was born in 1955. I am a baby boomer, and this is the beginning of my story.

My Parents

My dad, Joseph John Buchko (Joe) was born on August 29, 1924, in Ironwood, Michigan, as the fifth child in a closeknit family of six children. When he was two years old, his father was robbed by two men who took his money and then his life. To make ends meet, his mother did laundry and cleaned the homes of the wealthy. She never remarried.

From an early age, Dad learned to repair things and work around the house. He was athletic and, when he wasn't helping his mother, he was playing baseball, fly-fishing, and ski jumping.[2] When WWII broke out, Dad enlisted in the Army and, as the war drew to a close, he was called upon to fight near the Battle of the Bulge which took place in Belgium and lasted from December 16, 1944 until January 25, 1945. The timing of this battle meant the soldiers fought in frigid weather conditions including freezing rain, thick fog, deep snow drifts, and record-breaking low temperatures. There were more than 15,000 reported cold injuries from trench foot, pneumonia, and frostbite. Dad wasn't prepared for the bloodshed or facing the loss of so many comrades and, after the battle, thousands of men, my father included, were sent home emotionally scarred for life.

My mother, Patricia Mae Osterberg, was born on May 16, 1929, in a modest home in Ironwood, Michigan. She was the second born in a family of four children. Like most families, incomes were modest, and my mother's family struggled to make ends meet. Their oldest child, my mother's older sister, Betty Lou, was sickly. Because her mother, Flo, liked to party all hours of the night, my wealthy great-grandparents took my aunt Betty Lou to live with them in Hollywood, California, hoping the warmer weather would be good for her health issues.

When my grandparents struggled to find work in Ironwood, they announced their plans to move to Van Nuys, California for a new start where jobs were plentiful and where they could be closer to their oldest daughter, Betty Lou. Perhaps Grandma Flo wanted to be near her parents to remind them of her inheritance. [3]

Tumultuous Times

After my dad, Joe, came home from the war and met my mother, they started dating but their relationship was tumultuous. Mom's Spanish blood brought about a serious temper and sharp tongue that could carve up the toughest of men. After a heated quarrel, my mother decided to move west with her family and had no qualms about leaving my father in Michigan.

One of my dad's many dreams, and perhaps his biggest, was to live in Alaska so he could embrace the outdoors and fish in its mighty rivers. Despite wanting to fulfill that dream, he missed my mother, so instead of Alaska, he headed to California. After several months with her and one doozy of a fight, he decided to hitchhike to the land of his dreams. Having no money, he only got as far as Roseburg, Oregon where he eventually landed a lineman job with Pacific Gas and Electric.

Life without my mother proved to be lonely so he took a huge leap of faith and asked for her hand in marriage. They were married on November 17, 1948, and, before long, they purchased five acres outside the city and began building their first and only home together with hopes of quickly starting a family. My father built a three-bedroom, one-bath home from the ground up, including the plumbing and electrical work. He built a large deck across the rear that backed up to a large hill loaded with oak trees and he added a deck across the front of the house.

Starting a family wasn't as easy as they had hoped and anticipated. They went for fertility testing and were perplexed when the results showed they were both favorable for having children. With many failed attempts, my mother became extremely depressed, and every day became a struggle. After five years of trying, they became pregnant and my brother, Steven Jeffrey, was born on September 11, 1953. I came 19 months later, and though they wanted to keep adding to the family, I was their final child. (Years later when mom had a hysterectomy, the doctors told her that her tubes were so narrow, it was a miracle she was able to carry and give birth to Steven and me.)

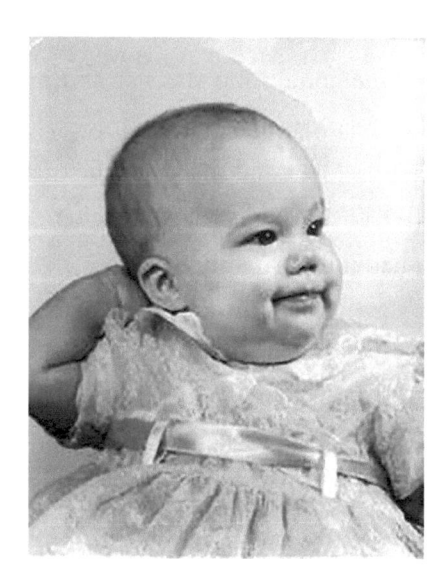

Figure 1 My baby picture

Life in Roseburg[4] was a simple one for the Buchkos. Each day Dad went to work while Mom cooked, kept house, and sewed. Although Mom wasn't a particularly good cook, she was a master at baking bread. My brother and I would fight over the ends of the bread when it came out of the oven, slathering fresh butter on our special piece of heaven. Dad hunted deer and elk to put meat on the table, and he and Mom fished along the shores of the Umpqua River for Steelhead salmon. Mom learned to can fresh food from the yearly garden, which included green beans, corn, tomatoes for making sauce, and cucumbers for wonderful pickles.

Working at the power company in Roseburg provided Dad with an opportunity to produce a good income. He started as a lineman and went to classes to become an estimator. Over the years, he turned down advancement opportunities because he put family first and wanted to be home at 5 p.m. Being available to us was important to him, and there is no price that can be put on the sacrifice he made to be present with us, especially during our childhood. Yet, as growing up goes, there were times when Dad was at work when I needed him with me to serve as my protector and guide.

My growing up years were based in a home where tempers flared, insults were hurled, and my healthy self-esteem threatened my mother's ability to control me.

My growing up years were based in a home where tempers flared, insults were hurled, and my healthy self-esteem threatened my mother's ability to control me. Journey with me through the next chapters as I present a sampling of my tender childhood years. I write these things not to dishonor anyone, but to give an honest view of the backdrop of how I grew up.

Keep in mind that, after all was said and done, this book is about unconditional forgiveness and healing. To paint that picture, I need to first walk you, dear reader, through the pain, scarring, and depth of many emotions that had to be worked through and surrendered to Christ!

CHAPTER 2

Emotional Distress

Emotional and Verbal Abuse

We often visited Mom's family in California, which was a fifteen hour drive, and we stayed with my aunt Betty Lou who lived in Hollywood. Grandma Flo lived in Sherman Oaks, and my uncles lived in Van Nuys and Glendale, which is where we usually gathered.

During the summers, I spent time with aunt Betty Lou and visited Grandma Flo, who was far less than pleasant. If I had an ounce of self-esteem, she would obliterate it. She was controlling, temperamental, dramatic, and verbally abusive. She teased me about my weight, and she was constantly annoyed by my ability to focus on multiple things, which somehow triggered her anger. Though never diagnosed, I grew up with Attention Deficit Disorder and, as a child, I had an uncanny ability to memorize numbers which caused her to think I cheated at board games.

I learned to escape deep within myself to calm my anxiety and keep my sanity.

One summer as she and I were playing Cribbage, a baseball game was on television.

Without any problem, I followed the details of the game as we played. She was so angered by this that she threw the cards at me while accusing me of cheating and, at the top of her lungs screamed, "I will never play cards with you again!" On another occasion, she insisted on teaching me the fine art of pie making, but just like the card game, she became irate and screamed, "How dare you multi-task while you are learning to make a pie." She then ordered me out of the kitchen. As one can imagine, we were never close.

Except for my aunt Betty Lou, I found my mom's family to be difficult and challenging. There were moments that were tolerable, but when the heavy drinking and conversations about politics and religion started, it was more than chaotic. I learned to escape deep within myself to calm my anxiety and keep my sanity.

One Christmas Eve when I was six years old, an argument erupted between my mother's siblings and Grandma Flo. What followed was vicious screaming and yelling, name calling and swearing. I was terrified that someone would physically lash out at a family member. Before long, presents were snatched from under the tree, thrown into the yard, and everyone piled into their cars and raced off. Watching the pandemonium was traumatic.

Emotional and Psychological Issues

Some would say my parents had a tumultuous love/hate relationship, but I don't agree. Their fighting made me nervous and frightened. Each time they screamed and yelled at each other, or when my father stormed out of the house slamming the front door behind him, I feared he would never return. Sometimes I believed their fights would suck the oxygen out of the room. Dad always came back, but I felt a sense of abandonment each time it happened.

Aunt Betty Lou came to visit one year, and an argument broke out. We were enjoying pizza, something he chose not to eat, so he decided to cook himself an egg. For whatever reason, my mother was upset that my father left a spoon on the stovetop, saying he never picked up after himself. He banged the spoon on the stove, stormed out the door and slammed it so hard I'm sure it was heard a mile away. I started crying and my brother tossed his pizza across the table. It took a couple of days before our parents were on speaking terms again. These events were not weekly occurrences, but we never knew when the next blow-up would happen. Their fighting had a negative impact on me and, because I was extremely sensitive, the expectation and fear of the next fight affected me from a psychological perspective.

As I grew up, I became close to my father. He was a humble and kind man and, because he grew up without a father, he wanted to be a good dad. Every Saturday morning, like a kid, he would sit with me while we watched cartoons. My favorite was Sylvester and Tweety Bird. Alas, the nickname my father gave me, until the day he died, was Tweet. On Saturday afternoons, Dad and I would take a nap. It was really my naptime, but he said he needed one too, so the two of us would snore away for an hour or so.

As I grew into a teenager and started dating, it seemed each one of my boyfriends became close friends with Dad. When I broke up with a boyfriend, it was not unusual to come home with a new boyfriend and find one of my former boyfriends spending time together with Dad, working on the car or involved with some other project. It was embarrassing. As I grew older, I realized Dad was a father to many of our friends, which was one of the many things I loved and admired about him.

As for my mother, from morning until night, she was the matriarch, and she made sure everyone knew she was in charge. She controlled everything in my world, but she was not sensitive like me, so she didn't understand my needs as a child, nor did she understand why I couldn't simply move on from a painful situation and forget it happened. Mom had been raised in a home with no affection, so it was rare to receive any from her.

From the time my brother Steven was born, he had a bad temper, a solid stubborn streak, and he fought my mom and dad about everything. Because he was the firstborn, my parents doted on him. He and my dad were both athletic and spent many afternoons in the yard playing catch. Steven learned to play baseball and football. Later, he learned to downhill ski and play golf. As we got older, his athleticism, strength, and stubborn streak became useful in his desire to be protective of me.

The Buchko Family

Almost every summer, we would get in the station wagon and head to Michigan to see the Buchko family. Dad liked taking different routes that took us into Canada and through many states. We camped out along the way and fished in the streams, and, if we were fortunate, we caught our dinner. Most of the time, I remember eating macaroni and cheese from a box, and no camping trip is complete without roasting hot dogs and marshmallows by the campfire.[5]

After arriving in Michigan, we spent most of the time at Grandma Buchko's. She lived in a big house in the heart of Ironwood with a large screened-in porch and a huge lawn. Many nights Steven and I would sleep on the porch and watch the fireflies and lightning storms. Grandma spoiled us with lots of ice cream and soda pop since we rarely got either at home. Each Friday night during our stay, we would go to the local bar for their weekly fish fry, a tradition handed down over the generations. At eight and six years old, Steven and I thought it was cool to walk into a bar and stay there to eat a meal.

While we were at her house, my grandmother made tasty pasties from scratch filled with meats, vegetables, and fresh potatoes. Over the years, Dad would make the same amazing pasties. The dough was light and flaky, just like a perfect pie crust, and he placed pads of butter on top of each one; this became his specialty.

9

When we left Grandma's, we headed to Wisconsin to stay with Dad's sister, Anna, who was married to Louis. They had a large farm which is where I learned to milk a cow, feed chickens, make butter, and, best of all, ride horses. Everything we ate was fresh from their garden or their fruit trees. Uncle Louis provided us with fresh meats and poultry and we enjoyed fresh cream and berries for our nightly dessert. But more than that, we enjoyed being with Aunt Anna and Uncle Louis because they were loving and supportive and made our visits fun.

Our little family also enjoyed weekends on the coast of Oregon, which was about a two-hour drive. We pitched our tent and threw our crab nets into the water. While we awaited our catch, we fished off the docks. Each morning we would dig for razorback clams.

When Steven and I were 8 and 6, Dad taught us to flyfish. We would head up the Umpqua River to catch Steelhead salmon. Dad was a master at flyfishing, casting his line at 10 o'clock, 12 o'clock, and 3 o'clock, and letting it go. He rarely walked away empty-handed.

On Christmas Eve, we would take a drive into the mountains. Mom would build a fire in the snow, and we would search out the perfect noble fir. After returning to camp, Mom would serve homemade hot chocolate, and we would roast hotdogs and marshmallows. Then we would strap the tree to the top of the station wagon and head home, where we would decorate the tree and then attend midnight mass.

"Then He adds: Their sins and lawless acts I will remember no more."
Hebrews 10:17

CHAPTER 3

The Fat Child

For the most part, Mom stayed at home with me and Steven until I started school. Then, she supplemented the family income by cleaning houses for the wealthy while we were at school. This was the perfect job for our family because she was home by the time we arrived in the afternoons.

As Steven and I grew, we kept ourselves entertained by using our long hallway as a bowling alley, exploring the wooded tree areas, and creating our own adventures. When I was six years old, Dad built me a miniature playhouse in the yard. I loved it so much that I would often fall asleep in it. I had many wonderful dreams in that little house of mine, many of which would never come true. And once I started to grade school, I stepped into a new world

I thought our home life was normal even though it was filled with activity that often centered around arguments, embarrassment, or ridicule. The chaotic drama was normalized early in my childhood because I was surrounded by it so often. Once I started

It seemed I was constantly placed under the spotlight of ridicule and pushed into a corner of loneliness, both at the same time.

to grade school, I came to know that these three things, arguments, embarrassment, and ridicule, were not just limited to my home, which should have been my safe place. At times, it seemed people from both home and school were set on destroying any self-confidence that may have accidentally found its' way into my heart and head. It seemed I was constantly placed under the spotlight of ridicule and pushed into a corner of loneliness, both at the same time.

When I was seven, mom invited some kids over to celebrate my birthday. One of the party games was bobbing for apples. Instead of allowing the party to be about the birthday girl, my mom placed herself front and center and bobbed for apples with the rest of us. I was embarrassed that she felt the need to be the center of attention, pushing herself into the spotlight, as if it were her birthday.

Then there was the issue of my stature. When I was young, I was told that I would lose my baby fat as I got older. That comment didn't make me feel better and I never did lose that baby fat. I often stared at the little fat girl on the Campbell Soup label and thought I looked like her, sometimes envisioning my face on the can. Even worse, people told my mother that I looked like that little girl. She was a towhead blonde, cute as a button, but fat. My parents told me I was cute, but I never saw myself as cute.

From the first through sixth grades, I attended a small school in the country. My classmates called me "Fatty Arbuckle," because my last name was Buchko, and "Big Fat Smart Fart," because I got straight A's. They also called me "Fat Country Bumpkin." My parents couldn't afford to shop at department stores so my clothes were homemade.[6] Under normal circumstances, I wouldn't care because other children also wore clothes made by their mothers, but my mom made crazy styles that accentuated my size, as if she wanted to make sure she looked better than me. This gave my classmates fodder to say things like, "She's poor, she's fat, and she has ugly clothes."[7]

To further crush my self-esteem, I had pimples and an awful overbite, which Mom called the Buchko bite. Though Mom said I needed to wear braces, we didn't have the money so her remedy was for me not to smile too broadly because my teeth would stick out too far, which was unattractive. And she said my pug nose was another Buchko trait, and it was too small, and on numerous occasions, she told me that I was "too sensitive," which was not meant as a compliment. Because Mom was a prankster and loved being the center of attention, I couldn't tell when she was teasing and when she was serious. Her words could be cutting and cruel and, when I asked if she were serious, she would laugh and say, "Of course not, I was just kidding." But the wounds from her words cut into my heart, leaving me feeling insecure and unloved.

As a child, I carried these negative comments from seemingly everyone and thought of myself as a fat, pimply-faced, bucktoothed, small-nosed, poorly dressed, overly sensitive girl. The only good thing I had going for me, it seemed, was my knack for school studies, multi-tasking, and numbers. To push down the pain and emotions of the constant bullying, rejection, laughter, and ridicule, I buried myself in my studies. I didn't know how to process the pain, so the scars stayed with me my entire life, buried so deep it would take an act of God to bring them to the surface.

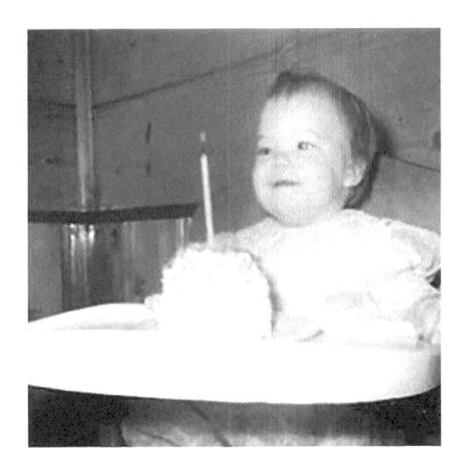

Figure 2 My first birthday, "Little Fat Girl"

Figure 3 My brother Steven and me

Figure 4 Sitting with the turkey

Figure 5 My first grade picture

Blooming Early

Puberty hit before anyone was able to educate me on the facts of life. Our school did not have sexual orientation classes, and the "S" word was never mentioned at home. In the fifth grade, I got my first bra long before most of the other girls, and I was ashamed of having to wear a harness around my neck. Though most girls long to have large breasts, I began to slump rather than hold myself up and sit straight. I wore high necklines in hopes that no one would notice them. I couldn't look at them in the mirror and I didn't like having to wash them. Having large breasts was another reason for kids to make fun of me, especially boys my age.

This wasn't the case for friends of my brother, who were older. When I was ten, two of the older boys decided I would be a good test subject. They wrestled me to the floor, pulled up my top, and began feeling my breasts to see if they were real. When they were finished, they laughed and left the room with me still lying on the floor. This was humiliating, frightening, and degrading. When I was eleven, another of my brother's friends grabbed my breasts and blurted out, "These are really real!"[8] I was ashamed. I blamed myself, and I hated my breasts because they seemed to be another burden I had to carry. And again, I didn't know what to do with these feelings of shame, blame, and guilt. I didn't know how to process the humiliation of what had happened and what I did wrong. So I pushed it all deep into my psyche, which was layered on top of everything else that had happened up to this point in my short lifetime.

Then there's the issue of my period. My mother prewarned me saying, "Don't be afraid when you get your first period. You will see some blood, but it's all in the natural course of life. It means you are transforming into a woman." I don't think she believed I would start menstruating in the fifth grade, because ten and eleven year old girls are considered young for starting puberty. It wasn't even on my radar.

Then, one evening I went to the bathroom and there it was staring at me from the toilet bowl – the evidence of graduating into womanhood. I called the bowling alley, where Mom was out for the evening, to tell her the good news. I was excited, but I could tell she was shocked. This wasn't the first or last time I would shock her. My excitement faded quickly because my period was accompanied with extremely painful and wicked cramping, which I thought was normal. I wondered how every transformed woman experienced this much pain every month without complaining.

CHAPTER 4

Glory Days

My mother and I went to see the movie, *Guess Who's Coming to Dinner*, which is about an interracial marriage between a black male and while female. On the way home, I told my mom how handsome I thought Sidney Poitier was. She went into a rage, saying if I ever brought home a black boyfriend, I would be kicked out of the house and not allowed to return. Then she forbade me from dating anyone with black skin, noting that black and white does not make a good mix. It seemed she wanted to push her prejudice onto me so that she had control of my love interests.

Mom also wanted to control my weight. When I finished sixth grade, she took me to a dietitian who put me on a strict diet. I lost thirty pounds that summer. On the first day of junior high, with my long, blonde hair and a thinner frame, my classmates didn't recognize me. They thought I was a new kid! The ugly duckling had turned into a swan.

Entering seventh grade with a new look gave me the boost of confidence I needed to try out for the cheerleader squad. From the first time I saw cheerleaders on television when my father watched the Green Bay Packers, I wanted to be one. They were all pretty and I wanted to be pretty. I believed being a cheerleader would be a way to be accepted and fit in. When I found out I was chosen to be on the squad, I was elated.

Being a cheerleader taught me so much about myself. I found out that I was loud, which was important. I could do cartwheels, and I participated in any sport I could for the sake of getting exercise. I smiled and laughed a lot. I was in my element. Because I was hurting inside from the buried and unresolved wounds, I frequently faked the smile and laughter. I knew that appearing to be an energetic and happy girl was necessary in being a great cheerleader and accepted by other kids. I also knew that putting a smile on my face would get me the attention and acceptance from the students that I didn't receive at home. This was the beginning of learning to be a great actor. I thoroughly enjoyed being on the junior high cheerleading squad and hoped I would be chosen to cheer with the high school squad.

Entering High School

Glide High School was a small country school by the fork of the North Umpqua and Little Rivers in Oregon. Compared to other high schools, it was small and yet I was a small fish in a big pond. The girls who were interested in competing to be on the squad were popular, athletic, and pretty. Many of the girls could do the splits and Chinese splits. I was intimidated from the start, so each day after school, I practiced. I didn't think I would be able to master it because I had never been flexible. Yet, I believed that if I set my mind to it, I could do it, and I did, though I thought I was going to rip apart before mastering the splits.

When tryouts came for the varsity squad, I entered the competition. When I went to the gymnasium to tryout, it was packed with students. I wondered what I was going to do if I tried to do the splits and could only go halfway down. Everyone would laugh at me, but then, I had been laughed at all my life.

That morning, I, Vicky Leda Buchko, swallowed my fear, went onto the floor, and yelled as loud as I could with my award-winning smile and ended my routine with a perfect set of splits! Ouch! That same day, I was elected to the squad and was happy to become part of something that would help me meet and become friends with other kids, but most of all, feel accepted and pretty.

I was so proud the day I came home from school to tell my parents about earning a place on the squad. My father was excited and congratulated me. The school supplied one of my uniforms and the families had to supply a second one. My mother was upset that she had to make it, perhaps because she didn't want to make an outfit that would look good on me. She was simply not able or not willing to reassure, accept, or encourage me to reach for the stars. I had a growing suspicion that she felt like she was in competition with me, and she would do anything to hold me down so that she could continue to shine as the center of attention.

The squad went to every football and basketball game, and I learned every detail about those two games. My favorite was football.[9] I cheered at the top of my lungs during each game, I got along well with the other cheerleaders, and I quickly became popular. The kids all seemed to like me, most of the boys thought I was pretty, and I never had a problem finding a boyfriend. As I started dating, I was afraid to show off my big breasts and, because I was self-conscious, I didn't want any guy touching them. Many of my dates complimented me about my body, but I thought their words were either superficial or outright lies. I didn't think anyone would want me or my big-breasted body.

Figure 6 The high school cheerleading squad. I am on the right at the top.

In addition to being insecure about my overall appearance, I struggled with weight gain, though it was not to the same degree as when I was in grade school. When the pounds started creeping on, I learned to starve myself. For my small 5 foot 2 inch frame, I wore size 8 to 10 clothing, depending on the day, and food was a struggle as it seemed I could look at it and put on pounds.

Even though I was learning to manage my weight, my mother continually pointed out what she thought were my shortcomings. Perhaps this was her attempt to hold control over my weight and my emotional well-being. When I was fifteen, I started working at the bowling alley, keeping score for bowlers. I saved enough money to buy a pair of stylish bellbottom jeans. Before I could try on a pair, my mother asked, "Why on earth would you want a pair? You are too fat to look good in them."

> Words are powerful, they either build up or destroy, and emotional pain from so much negativity was tearing me apart.

She wouldn't let go of her need to constantly berate me. I often wonder if my growing self-confidence and popularity in school threatened her in some way. It seemed she took advantage of every opportunity to make sure I knew I wasn't good enough for her or for anyone else. During these high school years, I was rarely home for dinner because I worked and participated in several activities after school. My mother never recognized any of my achievements. Instead, she looked for ways to put me in my place. One night, I came home after dinner, so I heated a can of soup on the stove. My mother said, "You will never find a husband if you don't learn how to cook. You can't satisfy him with hamburgers and macaroni and cheese. No one will want you, that's for sure."

Words are powerful, they either build up or destroy, and emotional pain from so much negativity was tearing me apart. The rejection I felt was incomprehensible because I desperately wanted her to approve of and acknowledge me. On the inside, I was constantly crying from the never-ending pain of being ignored by her. I worked hard to make her proud; I was an honor roll student, the student body vice president, and a member of the cheerleading squad. I also managed the school newsletter and took difficult classes in a variety of subjects. Nothing I did seemed to change her heart toward me, and I felt continually rejected and unloved, which were emotions pushed deep down because I wasn't ready or able to deal with them.

At the same time, while my relationship with my mother stagnated, when I was a freshman in high school, Steven was a junior and we started becoming closer. We even learned how to tease one another in a positive way. One morning before school, I was sick and Steven was running late. Having only one bathroom in the house was sometimes a problem. I was feeling like I was going to throw up, so I ran for the bathroom. Steven didn't have a clue I was home so when I approached the bathroom, he came out as naked as a jaybird. I thought he was going to faint when I began to laugh. I teased him relentlessly about our encounter for the next couple of years.

This was also about the time he felt the need to watch over me, which made sense because he was a foot taller than me, standing at 6'2. At first, it felt odd that he was protective of me. But once I got used to it, I was thankful he wanted to take care of me. We began to talk at night after school, and I began to trust him with my deepest secrets. Many of Steven's friends were interested in me, but he kept them at bay, making sure I wasn't hanging around with the wrong guys.

However, in my sophomore year, a guy from California came to our school. My entire family seemed to like him, and feelings I didn't know I had started to surface.

CHAPTER 5

California Dreamin'

I didn't believe guys could be gorgeously handsome. When I was growing up, the adjective "gorgeous" was only meant for beautiful women. But make no mistake, he was simply gorgeous. This new sophomore transferred from California to our little Glide High School, and he stood out when I first noticed him at a school football rally in mid-September. Imagine a cartoon character who sees something surprising, and their eyes bulge out. That was me.

Paul was the rugged type with an amazing smile, hazel eyes, and dark blonde hair. He was tall and masculine with a figure that probably caught the eye of every girl at school. Paul was always uniquely dressed; he wasn't the typical blue jean guy, but he did wear jeans. His attire didn't include frills or embellishments, but he was a cut above the other guys at Glide High. I assumed it was because he was from California.

One day, I was on the basketball court with the senior rally team trying to subtly keep my eyes on him. It was hard not to look at Paul because his appearance was nothing short of eye candy. One of my not-so-subtle glances locked eyes with him – eyes that were staring back at me. From that moment, his eyes were bolted to me, and I gave up on the subtle glances and simply made the connection to let him know I was interested.

Before leaving sunny California, Paul was a fullback on the football team. Our coach quickly recognized his athletic talent, and before long, he had a position on the Glide High Wildcat football team as well as the track team.

The Homecoming game was electric, and our team provided the fuel that kept the excitement on a constant high. I was in awe with the moves Paul had. It was as though he was meant to make it to the NFL. But remember, I was a teenage girl with a serious crush on this guy, so perhaps my insight was skewed.

Our team won the Homecoming game and, the next night, the school held a Homecoming dance. I had butterflies in my gut hoping Paul would ask me to dance. I did know his eyes were on me a lot, which told me he liked me, or so I hoped. In any case, I arrived at the dance wearing my cheerleader outfit and my new shoes. My friends were there and we drank punch and talked about the game. After fifteen minutes, there was a tap on my shoulder. I silently gulped, hoping it was Paul, as I slowly turned around. It was him! He asked me to dance, and that was the beginning of a fairy tale scenario I thought could not happen in my life. We danced to almost every song and talked the night away. It was surreal. I finally learned what it meant when people would say they felt as though they were on cloud nine.[10]

I knew the night was winding down and I wanted it to keep going, but as the saying goes, "all good things must come to an end," and my perfect evening was ending. The last song began to play, and it was as though it was intentionally chosen for me and Paul. *Precious and Few*[11] by Climax started, and as it softly echoed throughout the beautifully decorated gymnasium, Paul held me close. We hugged each other as we moved slowly to the song. Paul took his right hand and softly caressed my left cheek when they sang, *"Precious and few are the moments we two can share."* That was the moment I knew we were destined to become a couple. I wanted the night to go on forever.

Shortly after the song ended, everyone slowly made their way to the parking lot. Paul held my hand as we walked outside, and it took every ounce of strength in my body not to melt away. We said goodnight and I got into my car and drove home as I replayed that wonderful evening.

After that evening, we were inseparable, and everyone in school branded us, *The Couple.* It didn't take long to fall in love with him. I was totally and without reservation head over heels crazy about him. Dating Paul, everything from my entire past that made me feel horrible was eradicated. Nothing from my past held me back or mattered anymore. For the first time in my life, I felt good about how I looked and about myself. My confidence level was at an all-time high and, to some degree, this came through in everything I did, including schoolwork, even biology, which I hated. I often fell asleep in class, but the teacher never seemed to notice!

For the first time in my life, I felt good about how I looked and about myself.

Paul's father was an accountant, and his mother was a stay-at-home mom. His parents were incredibly nice to me and held me in the highest esteem. Paul was an only child and the family seemed to move a lot. I never cared to ask about the reason for the many moves they had made.

My parents really liked Paul as well. Prior to him, I had boyfriends, but no one who made me feel the way he did. He had a certain something that made him special, and my parents treated him that way.

The first day Paul came to my home, we were watching a television program when my mother came in and sat in her chair, making the loudest, most obnoxious, and most inappropriate noise imaginable. I was horrified. Paul didn't laugh; he just looked at me. Before he or I could say anything, she returned to the living room, removed the whoopee cushion[12] from under her seat, laughed and left the room again. From that moment, Paul and my mother were good friends. When he realized it was all in jest, he thought she was hysterical and, of course, I thought she was not the least bit funny, but rather crass. My mother, the prankster, embarrassed me every chance she got, and I hated it.

Despite all that, Paul treated me with the utmost respect. He was intelligent, athletic, and handsome, not to mention he was fun to be with. He had an incredible sense of humor and could always make me laugh, and he often told me I was pretty. Imagine that! The once Fatty Arbuckle, the ugly duckling, was actually seen as pretty by the guy who had it all.

As *The Couple,* we did the typical teenager stuff like necking in the backseat, but I was old-fashioned and wanted to wait to have sex until I was married. That was, however, not to be the case.

On the evening of my seventeenth birthday, my parents were out for their bowling night. Paul came over to celebrate; one thing led to another, and my good intention of waiting until marriage suddenly vanished. Paul was beside himself. In a way though, I was sincerely happy because he was the man I absolutely loved and wanted to marry. I justified pre-marital sex and never had any regrets about our first time. In fact, it was magical. However, that first time was all it took for what was to come.

A month went by, and I missed my period. I wasn't sure what to make of it, as I had missed a period before, and missing a period is common for countless teenagers. I spoke to my best friend, and she said if I missed my period a second time, she would go to the clinic with me. The second month came and, once again, no period. So, one day after school, my friend went with me to the clinic to find out if I was pregnant, and I was. Who would have thought that the first time a girl makes love, she would get pregnant! I thanked my friend for being with me and asked her not to say a word to anyone.

That night, I decided to have the baby, and for the next week, I felt like a zombie. I would go to school, return home, and go to my room and try to find the right way to share the news with Paul and my parents. Paul kept asking what was wrong and it took me a week before I could answer. It was difficult to tell him, but as I tried to get the words out, he asked, "Are you pregnant?" Although he was shocked at my answer, he was supportive. We talked about aborting the baby, but my beliefs were strong, and no matter how small it was, it was still a baby.

Paul's solution was that we should get married, and though things wouldn't be easy, they would work out. We wanted to be together and believed love would find a way. Though we both wanted to attend college, a baby would change those plans, and we embraced the fact that marriage was the right answer.

The time came to tell my parents, so to lessen the blow, I told my mother first. She was furious, she screamed and cried, "How could you do this to me and your dad? How could you bring such shame to our family?" Then she was silent. When I tried to express my love for Paul, she silenced me by saying I was too young to know anything about love, too young to be pregnant, too young, period, end of subject.

When my father arrived home from work, my mother told him. While he didn't yell or scream, he spent most of the night crying. I called Paul to see how the conversation went with his parents, and he said we would have to talk the next day because he was grounded from using the phone. That told me we had a massive uphill battle ahead of us.

For five days, my parents were either silent, or they were weeping or outright crying. Neither spoke a word to me. I felt deserted and alone, as though I was abandoned as a worthless human undeserving of love. This seed of abandonment had been planted within my spirit many years earlier, but with each passing day of my parents not talking to me, the seed went deeper and deeper into the pit of my hidden pains and abuses, taking root as if to say it would never be released or driven out.

On the sixth day, my mother broke her silence and told me I should consider having an abortion, even though they had raised me to respect life. I objected vehemently and refused her suggestion, telling her there was no way I would allow anyone to talk me into aborting the baby growing inside me. I would not take that life away, no matter how difficult my journey might become. Even though I wasn't a Christian at that point, I knew abortion was wrong and I had no right to take a life that wasn't mine to take. A fetal heartbeat starts at about five weeks into gestation, and I remember hearing that, when the heart stops beating, this signifies death, so when there is a heartbeat, there is life.

Steven and I had grown close, and he became my knight in shining armor. When kids at school got nasty, he stuck up for me and nearly got into a few fights when kids made fun of his little sister's pregnancy. He encouraged me to do what I felt was right and not listen to the opinions of anyone else. He encouraged me to make my decision and never look back or wonder if I made the right choice. Those words helped me on more than one occasion. He was finally my big brother, my protector, and my friend.

On the other hand, Mom kept repeating that I had a college education in front of me and I shouldn't allow anything to distract me from that. I continually refused to have an abortion. I was determined that she would not control this decision. No amount of threatening, badgering, bullying, or abuse was going to force me to do anything to harm my baby. So she arranged to send me away to a maternity home to have the baby. She was insistent I would place my child up for adoption after birth. She did not want me to keep my child under any circumstances, and told me if I decided to do so, I would not be welcome in her home. She insisted that I follow her plan without question or refusal, and once I was home, the entire incident would be swept under the rug. Sweeping things under the rug was something I had gotten very good at doing, so this statement was probably the least threatening at the time. But it would also prove, over time, to be the most harmful and hardest to overcome.

Both Paul's parents and mine forbade us to marry, even though we pleaded with them to allow us that option and to keep the child. As our baby grew bigger in my belly, Paul came to my house to visit me several times a week before my parents shipped me off.

Being under my mother's control was difficult for most of my childhood, but her decisions about what I would do with this baby growing in my belly would change the trajectory of my life in ways I could not imagine.

"Lord, you are forgiving and good,
abounding in love for all who call to you."
Psalm 86:5

CHAPTER 6

Taken by Force

Early one Saturday morning, my parents woke me, telling me we had to leave for the Oregon-Idaho border where I would stay until the baby was born. They claimed to know a couple I was to stay with, but I had never met them. After a grueling eight hour trip, we drove up a long country lane. A woman named Ann came out to meet us. As my parents unpacked the car, Ann took me into a large house and showed me the room I would be assigned to for the next several months. It was a small room with a bed, a dresser, and one window. Though I was frightened beyond words, I forced myself to be brave and rest in my convictions that I was doing the right thing.

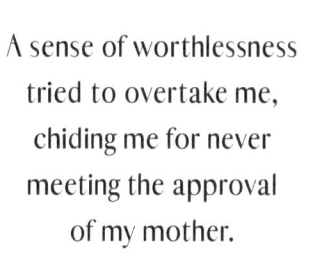

A sense of worthlessness tried to overtake me, chiding me for never meeting the approval of my mother.

My parents spent the night. The next morning, Mom came in to say she would see me after the baby was born and that I should write whenever I wanted to. My father came into the room and he was crying. He didn't want to leave me there, but he wasn't able to stand up to my mother in disagreement. He kissed me on the head, told me everything would be okay, and put a twenty dollar bill under my pillow for my pregnancy tootsie roll cravings. Then he kissed me and left the room.

I never felt more alone than when they left me there to have a child without their support. It felt like my baby and I were being tossed to the curb like garbage on pickup day. Being left by myself to give birth to a child I would not be allowed to raise almost suffocated me, like being trapped in a dark cave with a rock blocking the opening. Being abandoned in this place was worse than the doom and gloom of my Fatty Arbuckle days. Memories washed over me, reminding me of all the times I had felt abandoned through the years. A sense of worthlessness tried to overtake me, chiding me for never meeting the approval of my mother, and this being the worst thing of all because I had put shame on her. I knew her plan was to would abandon me here, punish me with her silence, force me to sign the papers to give away my baby, and never mention it again. And I knew she would control every aspect of everything she possibly could. How could someone be so cruel and heartless?

To make matters worse, the house I was left in was a modified maternity home.[13] In most of these places, there was more than one girl who was sheltered there. In this home, I was the only pregnant girl with no one to talk to about what I was going through, which only heightened my feelings of loneliness and need for someone to confide in.

About a week after arriving, my spirits were lifted when I got news that Paul was coming to visit. After he arrived, my spirits came crashing down at warp speed when he told me his parents had decided to move away so that we couldn't see each other again. I was devastated. Paul was my first and only true love, and I wanted the three of us to be together. Instead, the future looked incredibly bleak.

An overwhelming homesickness set in, and I asked my mother if I could come home for the weekend. Her answer was no because their friends from California were coming for a visit, and she didn't want them to see me in the state I was in. Instead of going home, I went to visit my best friend and her family. My girlfriend couldn't believe my mother's actions because everyone in our small community knew what had happened to me. Rejection hurts and can carve a deep wound within the heart. Left on its' own, it can wreak havoc on a life for an eternity.

Days seemed like an eternity in the maternity house situated in the middle of nowhere. I tried to stay positive and decided to focus on my baby. Even though I had no idea of the gender, I believed it was a boy. Every day, I took long walks and sang, *Somewhere Over the Rainbow.* Even as a seventeen year old, the song gave me hope that there would be an end to my pain.

One day when I was alone in my small room, I wrote a letter to my child, describing what I was being forced to do, saying something like,

> "No matter what, I loved you very much. I wanted to give you a good life, but without your father by my side, that would be a hard possibility. Just know, it was not my choice to give you away. My mother gave me no other choice except to sign you over to adoption."

I did have one family member who wanted to step in and help. Aunt Betty Lou offered to take the baby and raise my child until I was out of college and able to take care of the two of us. Mom wouldn't hear of it. She said she was ashamed of me and did not want a constant reminder of how I messed up and had a baby out of wedlock.

On January 9, 1973, after four hours of labor, my child was born. I heard the sound of crying and wanted to hold my baby so desperately, but this was not to be. The moment my child was delivered, it was taken from me. I didn't see the baby and I was not told whether I had given birth to a son or a daughter. I was cleaned up and sent to my room to recover. Recover? Was it to recover from childbirth or from the fact that someone had stolen my baby? Either way, being told to lay down and recover was pure evil.

The next day, my mother came into my room holding adoption papers. She told me that I was to sign them, and she literally forced the pen into my hand, saying it was too late to change my mind. Is this what happens to all young women in maternity homes? I did as she demanded, and then I cried all night, exhausted both physically and emotionally. Not once did my mother ask how I was handling everything. She simply handed me my clothes and said it was time to get on the road since it was a long journey. I had so much rage toward her, I thought I would explode at any moment, especially when she told me that I would have other children, and I needed to move on and never look back.

The eight hour drive home was brutal; no one spoke. I could see my father looking at me in the rearview mirror, and I could tell he was crying. I think he desperately wanted to say something, but he dared not with my mom around. I drifted in and out of sleep the entire drive, which was probably a good thing. When we arrived home, my mother walked me to my room, reminding me that we would never talk about my mistake again. She hugged me, said she loved me, and said I must move on. I was lost and couldn't stop crying, but my mother was having nothing to do with the grieving process. She kept repeating, "Don't cry. Forget about the baby. Push it aside, let it go, and move on."

The next morning, it took all the courage I could muster to get on the school bus. When I arrived at my first class, I was greeted with open arms. The acceptance from my classmates helped me realize I had done the right thing by having my child. After school there was a knock at the door and a delivery man handed me a bouquet of flowers and a box of candy. I thanked him and went inside to open the card. It was from Paul, who wanted me to know he was proud of me and would always love me. My heart was shattered. Between losing him and the baby, I believe I had a mental breakdown. In those days, people didn't talk about their feelings, and I certainly did not talk to my mother for fear of what she might do. Would she send me to a mental hospital? So, I held the pain for many years. My mind and heart blocked my feelings for both Paul and my baby. I was numb and had a difficult time relating to anyone, especially my mother.

I had learned to be a great actor while in junior high school, and now I was becoming even better at moving forward while burying my feelings. I thought about trying to find Paul, though I had no idea where he moved. My mother threatened that, if I did try to find him, I would no longer be welcome at home. She was successful in controlling me with this particular threat because she knew I had nowhere else to go. Paul must have heard the same thing from his parents because he and I had loved each other, yet he never tried to contact me.

Thoughts of Suicide

Shortly after having the baby, in the midst of my mental breakdown, I went into a state of depression, and didn't want to live anymore. Had I not been living with my parents, I doubt I would have gotten out of bed.

One evening I went to dinner with a trusted male friend and confided in him. Like almost everyone else, he told me to put everything behind me and move on. Why couldn't someone listen without giving advice? When we got in his car to head home, I tried to jump from his car, which was going sixty-five miles per hour. He grabbed the shoulder of my coat at the last possible second and dragged me back into the car, screaming at me as his car went off the side of the road.

Once the car was under control, he pulled over and screamed, "What in the world are you trying to do to yourself?" I told him I didn't want to live; I had no feelings left inside, no one really cared about me, and I didn't see a way out. We sat and talked for a long time. He listened, heard me, and his kind words of encouragement helped me live another day. I realize now that I just needed someone to listen to me, allow me to grieve and process, and validate that I was worthwhile. I am always amazed how the listening ear of someone who cares can right a multitude of hurts and be a healing balm to soothe even the deepest wounds.

The Senior Prom Court

When I returned from the maternity home, I was in my senior year in high school. One day, my favorite teacher asked if I had a date to the prom. When I said no, he advised me to get a date because the junior class had cast more votes for me to be on the prom court than anyone else. He said if I didn't get a date, he would be honored to be there with me. As soon as my mother caught wind that I was elected to prom court, she became interested, but it wasn't for the reason I thought.

On prom night, a close friend from another school went with me. It was fun showing up with him because nobody knew him. We were there for about fifteen minutes when one of my friends asked me if I was aware that my parents were hiding in the corner. Were they there because they were proud and wanted to enjoy the moment? Knowing my mom and her selfishness, I knew she was there because she wanted to live the moment through me. I was horrified because no other parents were at the senior prom, hiding in the corner, waiting to see if their daughter received the crown. How like her to want to be the center of attention at my event, and to show up unannounced. Embarrassed, I asked my parents to leave, which they did. How could my mother, after all the pain and woundedness she had caused me during my pregnancy, show up at my prom and expect to, once again, be the center of attention? Her actions only forced me deeper into depression and confirmed the belief that she was in competition with me, determined to rob me of any joy I might have.

Mom kept her word about never talking about my baby. She firmly believed in burying things under the rug. I thought about looking for my child many times after birth, but I chose to wait until my child was old enough to understand that he/she was adopted.

"And when you stand praying, if you hold anything against anyone, forgive them, so that your father in heaven may forgive you your sins."
Mark 11:25

CHAPTER 7

Believe

At the age of eighteen, I moved to Eugene, Oregon for college. At that stage of life, I was still suicidal most days. I ate like there was no tomorrow, and I went from size 8/10 to size 14/16. Sadness and depression can do that to a person.

To feed my sadness, my college friend and I would go on bike visits to Milk Farm, a dairy close to where we lived, and I would buy a half-gallon of German chocolate cake ice cream. Then I would peddle home and eat the entire carton in one sitting. I ate popcorn with lots of butter, McDonald's Big Macs, and M&Ms. One day I walked into a clothing store and couldn't fit into size fourteen. I knew I had a problem, but I couldn't stop eating junk food. I was hooked and I was huge. The weight gain further fueled my low self-esteem and my self-hatred. I needed to forgive myself for hating my body. Not until I forgave myself, would I be able to lose weight and move forward. With the grief in my heart and the

With the grief in my heart and the sadness weighing me down, I didn't know how to do anything except walk through the motions of everyday life.

sadness weighing me down, I didn't know how to do anything except walk through the motions of everyday life.

To add to my hopelessness, my mother gleefully and smugly told me that she heard Paul was engaged to be married. That news sent me further into depression. I believed my baby was in a better place, being cared for by adoptive parents, but I didn't stop missing my baby or thinking about the life Paul and I could have had together. I grieved the loss of both of them for several years.

Then, to add weight onto my already heavy spirit, my mother made me a baby blanket using fabric with images of a hippopotamus. This was one of my favorite animals as a child, probably because of how heavy and cute they were, and due to my weight issues as a child. She said, "Put this in your hope chest because you will use it one day." How she could be so insensitive? Didn't she know I had lost all hope and no longer believed in happily-ever-after?

My college friend encouraged me to accompany her to a new non-denominational church, Eugene Faith Center. I laughed when I entered the church because their services were held in a gymnasium, unlike my past experiences attending the Catholic church, which held their services in beautiful building with statues. This church still had basketball hoops hanging in four locations. We sat on the bleachers and in the center of the court was a platform where the worship team would gather and the pastor would preach.

Pastor Roy Hicks and Faith Center were an outreach of Church on the Way in California. I was immediately comfortable and entered into worship by singing songs mostly created from scripture. It was as if I'd known the songs forever. At Faith Center, I could openly worship and express my love for the Lord without all the rules and regulations I experienced in the Catholic church, which was exactly what I needed.

Pastor Hicks was a natural speaker, and his messages spoke to my heart. I started attending twice a week. Looking around at my Christian brothers and sisters, they had joy in their eyes and hearts that I had never experienced. It didn't take long to discover the WHY of their joy – His name is Jesus.

One Wednesday night shortly after I started attending Faith Center, the elders stood at the front of the church and asked if there was anyone in the congregation who had never accepted the Lord into their heart. They invited us forward, saying they would pray for anyone who wanted to meet Jesus. I didn't hesitate. I walked to one of the elders and asked him to pray with me to accept the Lord into my heart.

That night I met Jesus for the first time. I received inexpressible joy and peace. For the first time in my life, I was happy! When I met Jesus, I found love and acceptance through Him, but that didn't mean the feelings of abandonment disappeared overnight. That journey would take a lifetime.

"For God so loved the world that he gave his only Son, so that everyone who believes in him may not perish but may have eternal life. Indeed, God did not send the Son into the world to condemn the world, but in order that the world might be saved through him."
John 3:16-17

The Storm is Upon Us

"When I was a child, I talked like a child, I thought like a child, I reasoned like a child. When I became a [wo]man, I put childish ways behind me."

—1 Corinthians 13:11

CHAPTER 8

Deadly Tongue

After giving my heart to the Lord, He started transforming my heart to make me new. One of the first things He pointed out was a generational sin handed down through my mother's family. What was that sin? You guessed it – a deadly tongue. As a child, I learned from the example of my grandmother Flo and mother how to use my tongue to inflict pain. And as a child, I learned to walk in this generational sin and live out what I had been taught. I perfected it by using it against my brother. We didn't have a great sibling relationship, as teasing and cutting remarks were something he and I learned at home at an early age. I knew how to tease my brother and make him angry, and I did this more times than I can count. Both of us were good at hurting one another deeply with both our words and our actions.

By the time I was a young adult, I had mastered the fine art of teasing with such a cutting edge, most of those around me did not know when I was teasing and when I was serious. I also had a sharp tongue, which I used frequently to cut down people I didn't like. I was a quick thinker, so no one could keep up with my wicked tongue. I used it as a weapon to hurt others, and those wounds I inflicted were far more damaging than if I had inflicted physical pain.

In writing my story, I can see more clearly how I was doing the same thing to those who had bullied, ridiculed, and mocked me in my early childhood and grade school years. At times, I had to ask my mother if she was serious or teasing and now, I was inflicting the same kind of tone and insults onto others. As a child, it seemed people enjoyed cutting me down, and as a young adult, I took pleasure from making others feel worthless and less-than. Ill words had cut deeply into my heart from the time I was a young child, and because I buried those words and ignored the wounds, they were manifesting into behaviors that mirrored what others had done to me.

Years later, Cher's hit song; *"If I Could Turn Back Time"* woke a lot of people up to the reality of hurtful words when she sang:

> Pride is like a knife, it can cut deep inside
> Words are like weapons, they wound sometimes.[14]

In my twenties, as hard as I tried on my own, I found that I couldn't always control my vile tongue. I hurt a close friend with words that no one should even whisper. Later that night, I felt bad and asked for her forgiveness but realized I had a much larger problem. I knelt and asked the Lord to silence my tongue from that night forward. I didn't want to use its sharpness to hurt another human as long as I lived, even if they hurt me first. I wanted the ability to remain silent and not retaliate toward the person who hurt me.

God's plan was to return me to the woman He created me to be before He formed me in my mother's womb and before the attitudes and sins of the world were entrenched within me.

I believe prayers are answered when we pray from a repentant heart. I received an answer to my prayer. To this day, thirty plus years later, I cannot speak words to retaliate when others hurt me. The words do not form, and my tongue remains silent. This doesn't mean I'm not mad inside, but I cannot use my sharp tongue to retaliate.

As it says in the Bible,

> *"Thou shalt not avenge, nor bear any grudge*
> *against the children of thy people,*
> *but thou shalt love thy neighbor as thyself: I am the LORD."*
> Leviticus 19:18

And, as always, God's timing was perfect. Had I walked through the next season of my life with this generational sin hanging over my head, I would have continued to use it as my choice weapon to strike out at others when I was faced with pain, insecurity, abandonment, and despair. But He had better things in store for me. His desire was for me to learn who He is, to walk in His ways, and to gain strength in my heart, spirit, physical body, and resolve.

His plan was to return me to the woman He created me to be before He formed me in my mother's womb and before the attitudes and sins of the world were entrenched within me. But being remade doesn't come without walking through some storms. Unlearning behaviors, exposing the lies of the enemy, and setting things right often involves great shake-ups. But after a shake-up, things are renewed and look more like His DNA, which carries love, joy, peace, patience, kindness, goodness, faithfulness, gentleness, and self-control.

Put on your life jacket. We are headed into the storm.

CHAPTER 9

My First Marriage

One Sunday at Eugene Faith Center, a man named Dan sat close to me. He appeared to be a godly man, so I asked the Lord to let me meet him. The next Sunday, Dan had it worked out. At every worship service, the congregation was invited to introduce themselves to people they had not met. I turned around and right behind me was Dan and his friend, Tom. At the end of the service, I asked if they would like to come to the house I shared with my two roommates, Nanci and Cheryl. The guys accepted the offer, and the five of us had an amazing day, which went late into the night.

Dan and I started out being great friends. I learned that he was born in Green Bay, Wisconsin, and his family moved to Oregon when he was in his teens. He had six siblings, and his family did everything together, which was amazing to see, yet difficult for me because I wasn't raised the same way. I didn't like sharing Dan with his family all the time,[15] but they expected it, and he wanted to please them, which was his way of feeling loved and accepted.

When Dan and I met, I was still heavy, but he was too, so it was easier to pardon myself.[16] The first time he hugged me, he felt like a big bear holding me. He was one of the warmest people I had ever met, and he had a great and giving heart and would give whatever he had to anyone in need.

There was always an attraction between us. One night after a church service, Dan asked me to dinner. We went to an Italian restaurant and shared calzone. After knowing one another for six months, Dan and I officially started dating. We became inseparable.

After our engagement, my mother gave her opinion of our relationship. She said she never liked him, and if I married him, I would never amount to anything. Maybe she thought her negative words would keep me from going ahead with the marriage. Maybe she thought she still controlled me as she had so successfully done during my growing up years. But I wasn't ready to hear her opinion, so I buried it much like I buried everything else I wasn't ready to deal with.

After we were married, we bought our first home in Eugene. We worked through the first year of getting to know one another better, and we worked to apply those things we thought would make us a strong and happy couple. Because of the times and our upbringing, we believed the man was responsible for managing the finances, assuming the man was the provider for the family, and generally made more money. I faithfully put my paycheck in the bank every week, trusting him to take care of our financial obligations.

In the late 1970s, after selling our home in Eugene, we headed to Fair Oaks, California with a boat, three cars, and a wonderful future ahead of us. We purchased a small three bedroom, two-bath house with oak trees, which I loved, and a pool in the backyard. The house was a fixer-upper, but we didn't mind. I was resourceful and knew how to decorate and transform a house with little money and a great imagination. I was proud of our endeavors.

I was also proud of my efforts to transform my body. Diets were a regular part of my life until we moved to California, when I stopped eating and dropped to size four. If I felt like I had gained weight, I would starve myself for days like I had done in high school. My self-esteem was so tied up in my weight, I felt to be better accepted and have friends, I needed to not be known as the FAT girl in town.

About a year later, we began hosting Bible studies in our home. We had over thirty folks crammed into our living room, so we decided to convert the two-car garage into a family room. Our Bible study friends pitched in and provided dry wall, paint, curtains, and carpet. It turned out great, and the studies grew in size. We hosted barbecues for the group and had pool parties with our friends from our new church.

During the majority of our marriage, I brought home more money every week than Dan. With both of us having jobs, I started to wonder why we were barely surviving, so I started looking at our monthly bank statements. There were withdrawals taken from our bank account each month that didn't make sense. When I confronted Dan, he told me he was lending money to Bob, who worked for him and had five children. Neither Dan nor Bob seemed to make money selling cookware, and Dan was giving money from my paycheck to help Bob feed his kids.

While I understood the gesture, resentment toward Dan and Bob set in. In a rather heated discussion, I told Dan that we could not afford to give money away – not to Bob or to anyone, and he agreed. My deepest fear was that Dan's habit of giving away our money in order to be accepted would destroy our marriage. Two months later, Dan took a job selling copiers, which seemed to go better for him, so he got Bob a job there too. Bob didn't make any sales, so again, Dan began giving money to Bob until he got on his feet.

Meanwhile, Dan and I had gotten further into debt. I was beginning to realize that Dan could not manage our finances. Bounced checks, overdrawn bank accounts, and maxed out credit cards became the norm in our household, which worried me because I had grown up poor and was afraid of being poor again.

When my parents would come to town, Dan would suggest going to dinner, but Dan never reached to pick up the tab, expecting my parents to pay. They became agitated and began to dislike him even more than when we met. In their opinion, not only was he not taking care of me, but he was also taking advantage of them. They saw him as a loser, so there was tension whenever they visited, which wasn't often. I became more resentful toward Dan because I was close to my father and, because of Dan, I didn't get to see him as often as I wanted.

Dan did the same thing with his parents. One Christmas, he owed them money and his parents decided that, instead of exchanging gifts, they would use the money Dan borrowed and had not repaid to pay down our debt. As everyone else opened presents, we sat in their living room with the family and watched. It was humiliating.

After moving to Sacramento, I went to work for a large construction company in their home office as the assistant to the VP of Finance. I worked long hours and when I went home from work, Dan was either volunteering at church or hanging out with one of his friends. I again faced issues of abandonment. At this time in our marriage, there was no time set aside for us to stay connected. Those old, deeply buried feelings of abandonment, loneliness, and worthlessness started to set in. I didn't feel important to Dan; I wanted us to spend quality time together, but that didn't happen.

My new boss and I hit it off from the moment I met him during the interview process. Our sense of humor was perfect for many laughs throughout the long days we spent together at work. I didn't look for a reason to have an affair; I simply wanted to be loved, supported, and desired. Work was my sanctuary because this man was smart, fun, and attentive. I fell into his arms.

I don't blame Dan for the affair. I was the one who found love and acceptance elsewhere. While the affair was short-lived, it was wrong. I felt guilt and shame and knew I had to tell Dan. When I did, his face turned red and there was a look of rage I hadn't seen before. He walked out of the house and moved into an apartment.

Frustrated, I decided Dan should not manage our finances anymore. Unfortunately, it was too late. One afternoon after coming home from work, a foreclosure notice was hanging on the front door. I sat on the doorstep and cried. What I didn't know was that Dan had been home earlier in the day and taken all the mail marked as late notices and hidden it. What I also didn't know was that Dan wasn't making sales. He couldn't cope with the pressures of the job, and he spent many afternoons at the movie theater to escape. Then he found other ways to escape when he started using drugs.

After I discovered the foreclosure notice, my life with Dan was in a downward spiral. I no longer trusted the man I married. He lied to me, and I wanted nothing more to do with him. When I confronted Dan about all he had done and kept from me, I realized we needed a separation. We would have to file bankruptcy, and we would lose everything, keeping only the clothes on our backs. My fear of being poor again was happening.

After the house and most of our belongings were taken, I moved into a small apartment with my dachshund, Heidi. It was a cozy place with two bedrooms and more than enough room for me, Heidi, and any guests I had over. It was a lonely time, though. I stopped going to church and spent most nights on my own. I felt like the Lord had abandoned me, and I did not feel true support from my church friends.

I lost my job at the construction company because of the affair and started a new job one month later. I lost that job because I couldn't focus on my work and kept making one mistake after another. I survived by drawing unemployment and using money I had saved that Dan knew nothing about.

I remembered how, when I was forced to leave home to have my child, I became independent. In many ways, I wished I had maintained that independence. When I took control of my own life and finances, it

Even through this brewing storm, I was reminded of my desire and need for love, acceptance, provision, companionship, and God's forgiveness.

was like a part of independent me was back. I no longer had the draconian belief that the husband was responsible for the family finances. I hardened myself to the pain that came along with not being able to trust my husband. I told myself I would never rely on anyone other than the Lord for the roof over my head and the food on my table.

Despite the separation from Dan, things started looking up. Then my car was rear-ended by a large truck. I was following the truck in front of me too closely, and when he hit his brakes, I ran into him, and the truck behind hit me, sandwiching my car between two trucks. The car was totaled, and I had whiplash and neck issues as a result. But I did what my mother taught me. She said, "Never express your feelings, just bury what bothers you and move on." So, I did, even though I was unemployed and without a car.

Even through this brewing storm, I was reminded of my desire and need for love, acceptance, provision, companionship, and God's forgiveness. These events unleashed a determination to live my own life apart from the control of my mother or the negligence of my husband. I found my own voice and learned to speak up for myself without using my deadly tongue. And I started gaining self-confidence in my ability to take care of myself. But these lessons didn't come without pain.

I hit rock bottom and wanted to die on many occasions through this storm. It was my deep relationship with the Lord that kept me going. And as much as I was unaware of what He was doing in my life, I did know that He was with me and I had a slight sense that He was proud of me, He loved me, and He wanted me to be free from everything that had held me captive for so long. The only way forward was with Him.

CHAPTER 10

Second Chances

When we are broken and don't deal with our inner hurts and wounds, they will surface and give us the chance to deal with them. In the past, I had continually squashed them deep inside. With the separation from Dan, things started to surface again, and I wanted to get to work and deal with some of the issues. I was tired of being broken.

One of the first things I realized was how angry I had been with my mother my entire life. She always expected me to push my feelings down, not talk about them, and keep moving on, and that's exactly what I did. The verbal abuse and the feelings of loss and abandonment were buried, and I had not dealt with any of those feelings toward her. My anger was so deep it had turned into a burning hatred.

One day, my mother and I were sitting by the ocean, taking in the beauty of the sea. I knew I needed to confront her so forgiveness could come. I began by saying, "Mom, I have hated you my entire life." She sat stone silent, acting like she didn't hear me. Then, in a strained voice, she replied, "What on earth are you talking about?" I explained, "I have never felt loved by you. You abandoned me and forced me to give up my child. You constantly teased me and put me down. Mom, I don't think you ever took an interest in anything I did unless it was something I wasn't good in, and then you ridiculed me."

Throughout my life, I had only seen my mother cry twice. Once when my father's brother died unexpectedly, and the other time when she found out I was pregnant. But as I spoke from the depth of my heart, she was crying. I said, "Mom, I want to forgive you and have a true mother-daughter relationship from this day on. I have thought about this for a long time and have processed through some of the hurt and pain from my past. I want to share some of these feelings with you because I want you to understand why I have hated you. I think expressing what has been buried for so long will help me heal and will help you understand who I am and what I need in a relationship with you." I continued, "Mom, throughout my life I have felt unloved, unwanted, and abandoned by you. Your words made me feel like I was a loser and would always be fat. In fact, you told me one day that I was fat and would always be fat. How could you say something

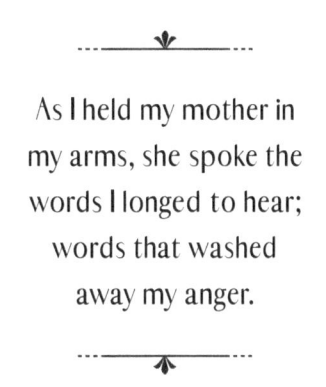

As I held my mother in my arms, she spoke the words I longed to hear; words that washed away my anger.

like that to your daughter? You had no words of encouragement, just shame. Another time, you said I would never amount to anything in life. Your words were, 'You can't cook or do much of anything else worthwhile to find a husband.' Mom, I didn't know I needed to cook to get a man to love me."

I paused for a second to take a deep breath. The deepest wound surfaced and I knew it had to be spoken so it could start healing. "Nothing I did ever got your attention until I became pregnant. Then I got your worst kind of attention. You demanded that I have an abortion and, when I refused, you sent me far away to have my baby on my own. How could you do that to me when I needed you the most? Then when you refused Aunt Betty Lou the opportunity to raise my child until I was out of college, that was the icing on the cake. I don't know how I could have hated you more over the years, but its' high time to forgive you and move on with a brand new start in our relationship."

As I held my mother in my arms, she spoke the words I longed to hear; words that washed away my anger and replaced it with love and tenderness toward her. Through tears she said, "Please forgive me. I had no idea that I hurt you so deeply for so long. I want your forgiveness and I want to wipe the slate clean and start over." On this special day by the sea, we did just that! We started over.

Another Second Chance

After ten months of separation, Dan approached me about trying to work out our marriage. He had a job in Eugene, Oregon and wanted me to move with him. I agreed because I felt strongly that it was my duty to make the marriage work.

We rented a beautiful house in the mountains surrounding Eugene. The house and location were serene and felt like my sanctuary. Though I had no experience in the legal field, I got a job with a small law firm. We returned to Eugene Faith Center where we met, and I began to believe that our relationship might heal.

Then Dan met a young man at work, and he felt the need to mentor him. Dan gave him money and a place to live – with us! The privacy we had shared was gone. The young man took every advantage. He didn't contribute toward rent, groceries, or even taking out the trash or clearing the dishes. Angered by having an unexpected and unwelcome houseguest, I told Dan to let his friend know he needed to find another place to live. Dan refused. Two months later, with the man still living under our roof, Dan announced he had been offered a job in Portland and would be going without me. He added, "Perhaps in a few months I might send for you."

The day came when he packed his clothes in his new 260Z and drove away in the pouring rain. I watched the movie, *Flash Dance*, sitting in a big chair, crying my eyes out. Another fear had come true; Dan's giving heart and his need to please others came at the detriment of our marriage.

I didn't stay in that sadness for long. My independence kicked in, and I was soon making new plans of my own. A couple I knew from church invited me to move in with them for a time so I could save enough money to move to my own place. I moved from my wonderful sanctuary on a hill into a large bedroom in their beautiful home. It was time to heal and start saving money. Each night, I returned to the loving, supportive home of my amazing and nurturing friends.

My best friend, Nanci, who had moved to Southern California, suggested that I move there and get a fresh start. It took me about six months to save the money and, with only the clothes on my back and my savings, I took a leap of faith and decided to move to Orange County, California.

I was ready to be a free, independent woman, responsible for only myself, and I had a sense that moving to California would lift a huge weight from my shoulders. And speaking of weight, my body was the thinnest and fittest it had been in my entire life. I worked out 5 to 6 times a week through various workouts. I ate clean food, rarely any junk at all and I hadn't put a MacDonalds hamburger in my mouth since college. Honestly, I didn't miss it and I felt so much better for it.

> *"For if you forgive other people when they sin against you,*
> *your heavenly Father will also forgive you"*
> Matthew 6:14

CHAPTER 11

Meeting Thomas

Before arriving, Nanci talked to her boss, Thomas, and told him that her best friend from high school and university was moving from Oregon and would be staying with her for a while. Thomas was the Vice President of Human Resources for a large, multi-state chain restaurant company that employed over 30,000 people. Their headquarters were situated in southern California.

Thomas was relentless to learn more about me. Nanci, his assistant, was circumspect and didn't share much, except that I was in the process of getting a divorce and I was small and athletic. She didn't share a photo of me or any other details, but the lack of information didn't stop him from inquiring often about my arrival.

Before long, I was in sunny California, starting a new life and looking forward to living with my best friend. One day I went to her office to meet up for lunch. After arriving, Nanci introduced me to the office staff. Then we walked over to a door, and she knocked. I heard a voice say, "I'm free," and we walked in. In his words, here is how he reacted at our first meeting:

"When Nanci first mentioned that Vicky was coming from Oregon, I had a strange feeling, like a premonition that

she was something special and that we were destined to be together. I didn't know why, but I was excited that she was moving to California. When she walked into my office that first time, what a feeling I had! I was so taken by this vision of loveliness that I could hardly speak. Vicky teases me to this day that I was afraid to look her in the eyes when I shook her hand, and she is partially right. I wasn't afraid, really, just overwhelmed with this feeling that the Lord sent her to change my life. The rest of that afternoon, I couldn't think of anything except Vicky."

The next day, Nanci scheduled to take the day off so she and I could go to the beach. That afternoon, she called Thomas to check on a few work related matters, and she casually mentioned that we were planning to have drinks that evening at a local pub. He asked, "Is it okay if I join you two after work?" I recall the expression on her face as she said, "Uh, hang on a sec." She covered the phone and whispered, "Is it okay if he meets us there?" I nodded my head in agreement.

Nanci and I were at the pub when Thomas arrived and slid into the booth beside me, which I thought was somewhat brazen. Looking only at me, he asked about our day at the beach. After half an hour of chit-chat and clearly ignoring Nanci, she excused herself to go to the girls' room. The moment she left, Thomas immediately took the opportunity to put his arm around me and pull me closer. I felt an instant connection to him. When Nanci returned, I could see a look of shock mixed with a sly bit of happiness in her eyes, as she noticed his arm around my shoulders.

The evening continued with no shortage of conversation between the three of us. Thomas seemed torn when he had to leave quite early, saying he had a prior commitment to help a friend install a rebuilt engine in his car. He said he couldn't put it off because he and his friend had an autocross race the next day in San Diego. As Thomas excused himself, I offered to walk him to his car. When we got to the restaurant lobby, there was a long line of people waiting to get in, and if I walked out, I would have to wait to re-enter. Thomas thanked me for offering to walk him to his car and gave me a kiss. With a cheer from the crowd and a few teasing remarks like, "get a room," we said goodnight.

Later that night, Thomas called and we talked until the wee hours of the morning. The next day, he was heading to New York on business. Since I had not yet secured a job, I had free time, so I bought him a few goodies for his trip and took them by his office to wish him well on his trip. He called every night from New York, and we talked for hours.

He was scheduled to return on Memorial day weekend, which would be a three-day weekend. He recalls,

> *"I had never asked a woman to go away with me for a weekend, but I somehow gathered the courage to ask her to go with me to Cambria, a small town up the coast near San Simeon and Hearst Castle. Without hesitation, and to my delight, she accepted the invitation."*

He sounded almost nervous when he invited me.

The drive from Orange County to Cambria was about four hours, and we talked non-stop about my childhood, school, family, my first marriage, my likes, dislikes, dreams, my faith in the Lord, my job search in southern California, and on and on and on. Likewise, I wanted to know everything about Thomas; his job, his failed marriage and divorce, his two daughters, ambitions, hobbies, interests, and his relationship with the Lord.

Thomas was an incredible man, and we had an incredibly wonderful weekend. Again, here are his words:

> *"On our trip to Cambria, I got to know Vicky. I knew without the slightest doubt that the Lord had sent this wonderful woman to become my wife and best friend forever. I only hoped that she would feel the same way. On our last night in*

*Cambria, we ate at a small restaurant in town. As we sat on
the patio and stared into each other's eyes, something strange
came over me – a warm glow and a feeling of happiness I had
never felt before. Without planning or forethought, I slowly
stuttered, 'Will you marry me?' I couldn't believe what I had
just asked! I had only known Vicky for two weeks and yet it
felt right."*

Without hesitation, to his surprise and amusement, I giggled a little
and replied,

"Yes. But what took you so long to ask?"

Skeletons from the First Marriage

At this point, the after-effects of marriage to Dan were not all reconciled.
Shortly after moving to California, I landed a job in a law firm. One
day at work, I learned that my paycheck was being garnished by the IRS
because Dan had not paid our taxes for seven years. Again, the walls came
crumbling down. Dan was now in my rearview mirror, and I realized I
needed to speed up the process of divorcing him before any more skeletons
jumped out of the closet. I made an appointment with a divorce lawyer
a few days later and had him draw up the papers. But before finalizing
the divorce, I went to Oregon to see Dan. I still cared for him, I believed
marriage before the Lord binds a couple for life, and I wanted to confirm
I was doing the right thing.

Dan hadn't changed at all. He continued to tell me that he would
make everything up to me and he wanted me back, but his words were
incredibly empty. When he dropped me off at the airport, I boarded my
flight and never looked back or regretted my decision, as difficult as it
was. With the Lord's help, I was able to forgive Dan and myself for not
standing and fighting back.[17]

I was headed home to California to begin my new life. Thomas and I planned to marry in the fall after my divorce was finalized, but as time drew near, I fell ill.

> *"If you do not forgive others their sins,*
> *your Father will not forgive your sins."*
> Matthew 6:15

CHAPTER 12

Hysterectomy

From my teen years through the time Thomas and I became engaged. I continued to have excruciating pain with my period. During a normal monthly cycle, I would be sitting at my desk, and when I would get up, my legs would be numb. It would take a few minutes before I could feel them.

The issue began to happen more frequently, so I decided to get medical attention. I had appointments with an internist and five specialists. The last doctor I saw was a neurologist who thought I might have a brain tumor. After numerous tests, I was informed that there was nothing wrong with me. The doctor advised me to seek psychological help because she believed the symptoms were in my head. I disagreed. I knew my body, and the pain was real.

The next month, I went for my annual female visit but to a new gynecologist, a man, and I had serious doubts I could trust him with female issues. My doubts were soon thrown out the window. He proceeded to ask about my history concerning my menstrual cycle. I think the descriptor, "excruciating pain," summed it up succinctly for him. I proceeded to tell him about the added symptoms I had suffered over the past year plus the specialists I had seen. I could tell he was disturbed by what I shared and could see sympathy in his eyes. Once I finished describing everything, he said, "It sounds like you have endometriosis." He never doubted me, and, like a knee jerk reaction scenario, I gave him the symptoms and he gave me the prognosis. He then explained all he knew about the disease, which wasn't much in 1984, and the symptoms that accompany it.

In order to determine if I had endometriosis, I would need to have a laparoscopy to see if there was evidence of it. If there was significant evidence, I would possibly need a hysterectomy. There was sufficient evidence, but the doctor suggested I get a second opinion. Because I was in my childbearing years, if I needed a hysterectomy, the hospital required two doctors to sign off. The second doctor confirmed I had endometriosis and agreed that I should have the surgery.

I felt as though I was in a vortex, as everything was happening so fast. My doctor scheduled surgery for the following week, telling me it would last about an hour unless they ran into issues. I had to sign a release form giving the doctor permission to perform a hysterectomy if the endometriosis was bad. I was so desperate to live pain-free that I signed it, wanting to feel normal and live a happy life every day, not just 21 out of 28 days.

The surgery lasted over four hours. The endometriosis was so severe that it had made its way into my uterus and ovaries and had attached to most of my major organs. The doctor said it was the worst case the hospital had seen. He added that it would have killed me if I had gone longer with no diagnosis. As I feared, all my reproductive organs had to go. This left me feeling empty. I had to face the fact that I would never have another child. I had been so focused on being pain-free and recovering that I didn't fully comprehend the final outcome of never being able to have more children. Once reality grabbed me, my brain went into tornado mode, spinning so fast with thoughts and emotions that flooded my every thought, and they were not good. I became extremely angry at the Lord and with life itself. Not only was I forced to give up a

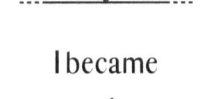

I became extremely angry with the Lord and with life itself.

child, but he or she would be the only child I would ever have. After losing my one child, I had eventually accepted the fact that there would be other opportunities for children. I was dead wrong.

I was so depressed I didn't want to get up in the mornings. Thomas had two daughters from a previous marriage, and he had a vasectomy and didn't want to adopt children. He would have adopted had I insisted, but I didn't want him to do that. Yet the thought of never having a child was emotionally painful. I always wanted to be a mother and thought I would be a good mother. But this wouldn't be an option unless I found my child who would be thirteen years old. I didn't think it would be fair to show up in his or her life and mess things up for my child. I decided to wait until his or her eighteenth birthday.

Each year became tougher. I was not close with Thomas' daughters and longed to meet and have a relationship with my own child. My biggest fear was that my child would either die before I found him or her or would not want to meet their birth mother. I cried myself to sleep more nights than I can remember.

We Tied the Knot

After I recovered from surgery, Thomas and I moved forward with our marriage plans. Autumn came and went, but that was okay because I had to get back to normal after surgery. On April 6, 1985, we were married aboard the Robert E. Lee paddle-wheeler boat, which was a floating restaurant moored in Newport Harbor. It was a clear but windy day, and Thomas had to pin my hat and veil to my head with more than ten hat pins. The ceremony was conducted on the bow of the boat, with the reception held at the restaurant inside. It was a small wedding with about fifty of our family and closest friends, including my parents. Even though it was a small wedding, our guests managed to drink forty plus bottles of champagne.

At one point during my father-daughter dance, I had my hand on my father's shoulder and could feel a large lump. When I asked about it, he said it was a cyst, and he got them on occasion. Though I let the comment go, I had an uneasy feeling in my stomach.

Thomas and I honeymooned on our wedding night at the Ritz Carlton in Laguna Niguel. Two weeks later, we flew to the Caribbean to enjoy a seven-day cruise. After a magnificent wedding and outstanding honeymoon the euphoric high of feeling life exactly where I hoped it would be, again came crashing down at freefall speed.

On our way home on the plane, I turned to Thomas and said, "There's something wrong at home, I just feel it."

Figure 7 My first wedding with Thomas

Figure 8 My mom and dad

CHAPTER 13

Losing My Parents

Thomas and I arrived home from our honeymoon at 11 p.m. and I immediately called my mother. My parents are normally in bed by 9, but she answered the phone, sobbing. She proceeded to tell me that my father had terminal lung cancer and had been given less than three months to live, which brought me to tears. I was devastated. I adored my father, and the thought of losing him was almost more than I could stand.

The next day, I boarded a plane and flew to Oregon to help my mother. I called the UCLA Medical Center to try to get my father help from the best doctors in the country. I spoke to a woman who asked where I was calling from. When I answered, "Roseburg, Oregon," she took a long pause and replied, "Your father will be in the best hands possible if he remains in Roseburg."

I found this a strange comment since it was such a small place. What I was about to discover is that three of the top cancer doctors from UCLA had opened a cancer center in Roseburg. I was elated and quickly shared this news with my parents. Within days, my father had an appointment in the clinic for his first round of chemo. It was truly a miracle. I called Thomas to share this great news and to let him know I would be home in a couple of days.

After everything was arranged, I helped my mom with some housework, pre-made some meals, then I headed home. I felt at ease that I did what I could to put my mom in position to help my father, and more so that my father was in the best care available. The emotional pain of my father having cancer was still there, but there was a sense of relief, and I was able to start my married life with Thomas. I would call and speak to my mom and dad daily to check on their progress with treatment. While the prognosis was grim, I kept praying for a miracle through the hands of these wonderful doctors.

Each day at the law firm was a struggle, but each evening at home, Thomas was there with his sweet, loving embrace, which made this horrible time easier. One day when I was at lunch, I remembered a conversation my mother and I had before Thomas and I were married. She said, "Vicky, I don't feel right physically. I can't pinpoint what is wrong, but I don't feel healthy." She then talked about how she wanted to be cremated when she died and have her ashes sprinkled over the ocean. My mom said that Dad did not want to talk about such things with her, so she wanted to make sure I knew of her wishes. I shrugged it off, acknowledging that I understood, and she was going to be fine. She never spoke of this conversation again.

When I called my mother one evening after work, I asked if she and Dad had spoken about his wishes for his body after he died. She said he still refused to talk about it because he did not want to believe he was going to die. He was choosing to fight the disease with everything he had. And fight he certainly did.

Thomas and I would talk about my parents every evening after work as we had our glass of wine. We would pray for my dear father who was suffering each night before we went to bed. I cried and wished I could take this burden from him. Each morning, I would head to work and keep as busy as possible so I did not have to think any further down the road.

Just as I became a bit more comfortable with my daily routine, I got a rude awakening. Three weeks after returning home to Thomas, at 3 a.m., the phone woke us. I literally jumped out of bed and listened to my brother Steven hysterically trying to get the words out. Immediately I thought my father had died when, in fact, he was calling about our mother. She had been rushed to the emergency room and was diagnosed with lung cancer, which was more advanced than my father's. The tumors were so large they cracked several of her ribs. The next few hours were beyond stressful. I had to try to think clearly, which was next to impossible, so Thomas helped me make the plane reservation and got me to the airport to head back to Oregon.

When I arrived at the airport, Steven greeted me. It was clear he had not slept in quite a while. We held each other and cried. He kept saying, "This cannot be happening." But it was happening, and we were in it together, so we got into his car and drove to the cancer center. My mother had been placed in the same facility as my father and was immediately given chemo and radiation to reduce the tumors, but she also had to stay in the hospital because of her broken ribs.

My father, Steven, and I visited her several times, but she was in intense pain on every occasion. Nothing helped. We prayed that our being there would bring some relief. The chemo made her sick, and she rapidly started losing weight. Radiation was no different. While my father was handling the chemo and radiation quite well, my mother didn't appear to be strong enough to endure it.

I helped my father by making some meals to put into the freezer so that the stress of meal preparation wasn't on his shoulders. I cleaned the house from top to bottom, and we spent many hours talking. He was sick, but he was at home, and he made sure I knew how happy he was that Thomas and I had married. This not only gave him joy, but as he said, was a good reason to battle cancer and keep living. His words gave me comfort in knowing he would be fine.

My parents' best friends were incredible and took Dad to and from his treatments. They reassured me and Steven that they would always be available for our parents to take them to their medical appointments. I could only stay for one week because I had to get back to my new husband and my job. Unlike my father, my mother was in the hospital for weeks. None of her treatment seemed to stop the cancer that was now spreading throughout her body.

My brother was a brave soul. Even though he worked more than a full-time job, he cared for our parents when their best friends could not.

Life can be so difficult at times. The feeling of being under water can consume us as we desperately search for that life preserver. I felt helpless, especially since I lived so far away. I made additional trips to see them, but my mother was not to live long.

I was blessed to have Thomas by my side, as he had so much love and understanding through the situation. We had only been married four months when all this was happening. Like most men, he wanted to fix the situation and move forward but he knew that wasn't possible. He held, hugged, and loved me. He also shed many tears for me. Sometimes I heard him praying that I would get through not just the imminent death of my mother but also for my father to combat his cancer. Although he was supportive, he was on an emotional rollercoaster as well.

Life can be so difficult at times. The feeling of being under water can consume us as we desperately search for that life preserver.

Mom had a tough time handling the chemo and she suffered more with the chemo and radiation than with the cancer, so she gave up after three months of treatment. I went to see her as they were moving her to a nursing home. Mom was frail and thin, but she still managed a big smile when she saw me for the last time. She told me she was happy that Thomas was in my life and was confident he would watch over and take care of me. Though it was a hard visit, I was thankful to see her. When I left, I kissed her and told her how much I dearly loved her. It was the last time I saw her alive.

To celebrate her life, we held a memorial service at the Catholic church we attended in my childhood. I gave her eulogy, which was difficult to do, but I wanted to make sure it was given by someone who knew her. My dad, Steven, and my aunt and uncles all contributed stories about her that made everyone laugh. She was the prankster of the family, so there was no shortage of stories. Her wish was to be cremated and her ashes sprinkled along the Oregon coastline. Dad wanted to wait a while before scattering her ashes because he was having a hard time letting her go.

After spending a couple of days grieving as a family, I had to return home. My parents had been best friends, and my father was devastated. He called me many times during the weeks that followed, crying, and grieving with me over the phone. It was hard not being with him to offer a hug and comfort. He was fighting for his life, without my mother, and he missed her terribly. When Mom died, he did not manage well without his true buddy. Dad spent his time creating stained glass, playing cards with his best friend, Floyd, and being with my brother and me. Without fail, Dad would get his chemo treatment, then drive non-stop to Orange County to see Thomas and me. Before long, we insisted on giving him a house key because we would find him in the driveway asleep in his car. His need to be with his family was paramount.

Thomas and I spent many great times with Dad during his visits. We walked on the beach, visited Catalina Island and other southern California sites, and hung out. We frequently spoke about Mom and his many memories of her. I knew how much my father loved me, a gift from the Lord, and he sure knew that his little girl absolutely adored him. For several months, we had so much quality time together, and both Thomas and I enjoyed every minute.

After almost seventeen months of treatment, my father decided his time had come to be with the Lord. His brother and sister had traveled from Michigan to see him. This was their first visit since Dad moved to Oregon over 40 years earlier. My aunt and uncle waited until he was on his deathbed to visit, which angered me in an unexplainable way. I kept thinking, "Why not come before he was on death's door and have a quality visit?"

My brother called late one evening and said, "Dad is waiting for you to get here to die." I was on the first flight I could get and, when I arrived, Dad was on the sofa with his eyes closed. I was afraid he had already left, but he had waited for me. I hugged him deeply and kissed his sweet cheeks. The ambulance was called, and I went with my dad to the hospital.

Steven and I were with him until 11 p.m., when Steven went home to get some rest. I stayed with Dad and dozed on and off. We talked a little as time passed, but soon his breathing was labored, and he stopped talking. Early the next morning, I climbed onto the bed with him because I could tell he was close to dying. He took his last breath about twenty minutes later, in my arms. I will never forget losing my best friend. The pain was so extreme I still cry when I remember that tender moment.

Steven and I spent the next day at the mortuary. Since Dad never wanted to talk about dying or arrangements, we picked a simple casket and found a small cemetery close to his house in Oregon. The lot was under a huge oak tree, and we buried him along with the remainder of my mother's ashes on a cold, sunny day in October. The deer were there to wish them farewell and to eat the fresh flowers that remained on the grave.

I lost my mother and father in less than seventeen months from when Dad was diagnosed. Anger welled within me. It was anger I had not experienced since the loss of my child and my ability to bare children. I wanted to know why the Lord took away my best friend, my dad! It was tough to let go of the resentment toward the Lord until I was able to move with Him over the rainbow and into the clouds of unconditional forgiveness.

Steven had never experienced a major tragedy before, and losing both parents was difficult for him. He stopped speaking to me for over six years. I wondered if he was resentful that I lived so far away and wasn't there to help him care for our parents. My attempts to communicate with him fell on deaf ears; he wanted nothing to do with me. The Christmas after the sixth year of not speaking, I sent him a Christmas card with a brief letter and the lyrics from a song, *"Grown Up Christmas List."*[18]

No more lives torn apart
Then wars would never start
And time would heal all hearts
And everyone would have a friend
And right would always win
And love would never end
This is my grown-up Christmas list.

Shortly after that New Year's celebration, Steven called and we talked for hours. We were on a journey toward becoming close again, but it would take years before we completely healed and became best friends.

"Be kind and compassionate to one another, forgiving each other,
just as in Christ God forgave you."
Ephesians 4:32

CHAPTER 14

Up in Smoke

After my parents passed on, Steven wanted the family house, so he gave me my half in cash. While it was not much money, it was enough to buy a small house on a cliff by the ocean in Gold Beach, Oregon. Prior to the purchase, Thomas and I had a geologist check out the stability of where the house was situated. We were told that each year, the ocean carves away a bit of the cliff. However, he did not see any issues for the near future. I was excited to purchase this small house – even Thomas liked it. We wanted to eventually renovate it and use it during our retirement.

We decided to rent it out full-time until we could afford to reserve it for our use only, hoping that would be two or three years. Those hopes were dashed when, late one evening, Thomas and I received a call from our tenants who told us that, thirty minutes prior, it felt like an earthquake had shaken the house and the entire cliff below had eroded, positioning the house on the edge of the cliff. However, what actually happened was earlier in the day there had been a horrific storm and huge storm surge. The storm surge had eroded the entire face of the cliff below the house and the house was dangling precariously off the edge.

It took days for this to sink in before Thomas made the trip to Oregon to assess the damage. I was too emotional to go, not wanting to face something else taken from me. I cried, "Lord, not again! Why can't I have dreams of my own that come true?"

Thomas called me later that evening to let me know the house had to be demolished because there was not enough land left to move it back. I asked whether we had enough land to build another one and he answered, "No. The entire cliff collapsed. It's truly unbelievable." In addition, we had received a notice from the State of Oregon advising that if the house fell down the cliff and onto the beach below, we would be responsible for the beach cleanup costs.

When I heard this, I cried until I thought my eyes would swell shut. Again, my anger turned toward the Lord. I didn't speak to Him again for a long time, and I didn't pray. Although worse things had happened in my life, this was one of the most emotional times I experienced. With the hysterectomy, I lost the dream of having children. Then I lost my parents, and I lost my dream home. How could the Lord do this?

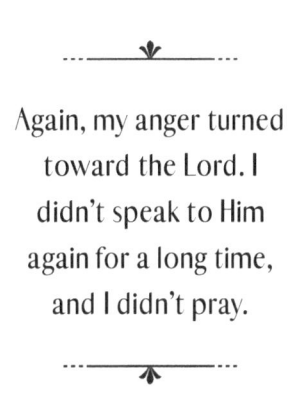

Again, my anger turned toward the Lord. I didn't speak to Him again for a long time, and I didn't pray.

Two days later, at our request, Thomas watched as the fire department burned the house to the ground. My dream went up in smoke.

Adopted Mom

After my parents died, their best friends became my family. While Mom and Dad Haas never legally adopted me, I felt like their daughter, and they treated me that way. Mom Haas was everything to me that my mother wasn't. She was supportive and loving on all levels. She gave great advice but then allowed me to make my own mistakes. She greeted me with hugs and kisses and encouraged me and told me how special I was. She called me her angel.

Whenever I visited Oregon, I stayed with my adoptive parents. They took me under their wing, and we did everything together, like cooking, canning, playing cards, drinking, and fishing. She taught me how to make her amazing "grammy rolls," which are homemade dinner rolls. We talked about my parents, she told me stories about her and my mother cheating my dad and Dad Haas in card games, and she said that whenever the boys would go the bathroom or make drinks, the girls would swap cards around so they would win. Whenever she was around, there was laughter and love. She was precious to be around and being with her helped me heal and recover. I wanted to spend as much time with them as possible, but our relationship was short-lived.

Two years after my father died, Mom Haas was diagnosed with lung cancer. She, too, had been a smoker for many years. I visited her every chance I could. On one trip, I was sitting at her bedside when the radiologist came in to check on her. He was the same doctor who had treated my parents, but I had never met him. Mom Haas asked him, "Do you remember Pat and Joe Buchko?" He responded that he did. She continued, "Well, this is their daughter, Vicky." His eyes looked into mine with tears and said, "I'm looking at the reason your father lived as long as he did. You were your father's miracle to live for." He told me that my father had a five percent chance of living past his three month diagnosis, but his will to live longer was that he wanted to see his daughter as much as possible. That will was so strong that he lived sixteen months before giving up. At that point, there was not a dry eye in the room. Though I knew how much my father loved me, it was wonderful to hear this story.

Mom Haas only lived for six months before she left this world to hang out with my mother and father. This was another major loss that was hard to deal with. It was horrible to live through more grief. I cried because I missed her so much, and again, my anger grew.

God's Rainbow Appears

"It is understood that the beauty of a rainbow does not negate the ravages of any storm. When a rainbow appears, it does not mean the storm never happened or that we are not still dealing with its aftermath. It means that something beautiful and full of light has appeared in the midst of the darkness and clouds. Storm clouds may still hover, but the rainbow provides a counterbalance of color, energy, and hope."

—Author Unknown

CHAPTER 15

Married Life

It seemed like an eternity, but our lives returned to normal. Thomas and I were both career-focused, working 50 to 60 hours each week. We bought a townhome and, later, a house in Dana Point, California. I loved to entertain and have guests over, and we had many enjoyable outings and dinner parties with friends. Life was treating us well, or so we thought.

After my mother passed, I wasn't as depressed because she and I were not that close. After the death of my father, there was no consoling me. I was able to get to work each day, but each night, I came home and cried.

The grief took its' toll on me, and the feeling of sadness lingered for weeks. I often thought it wasn't normal to be so depressed over the loss of my father for so long, and I hoped I would get better with time. I also knew my father would not want me to move on with my life until I was ready. But I knew that grief is an individual experience defined by the relationship with the person who passed on and the circumstances of their death. Although most bereaved people are likely to experience similar emotional effects of grief, their order and length depend on individual circumstances and the person's abilities to cope.

One night when Thomas arrived home from work, I was in the living room crying again. In a snappy, judgmental tone, he expressed, "Your father wouldn't want you acting this way, day after day. You need to move on." At that moment, I realized I had reached my breaking point and couldn't go any further until I grieved. Neither Thomas nor anyone else could understand my grieving process and as much as Thomas tried to help me, I knew I had to do it on my own. I responded, "I need to get away for a while and grieve without judgment or expectations of how I should act or perform, otherwise, we might have significant problems in our marriage." I knew he didn't understand, but I had no choice.

That night I packed a bag and temporarily moved to my girlfriend's home. I had a small room to come home to each night and grieve the loss of my father. Thomas tried to convince me to come home several times, but I knew if I went home too soon, our marriage would suffer serious consequences. I had to grieve in my own way and I could not go back until I was ready. Each day I would go to work and each night I would come home, lay on the bed, listen to music, pray, and cry. I rarely went out. Once in a while my girlfriend would convince me to get out for a walk or join her for a glass of wine. At least she knew that, in time, I would get over the emotional pain and be myself again.

Thomas and I would occasionally meet and have dinner. He wanted me to come home badly, but he rose to the occasion to give me as much space as I needed without again questioning my grieving process. Thomas loved my father too, even though he had only known him a short time, so he also grieved, but in a different way. To this day, I have moments when I miss my father and have a good cry.

After the three-month mark, I felt like I could go home and not feel judged by my husband or anyone else. Through this season, Thomas and I gained a greater understanding of each other.

From Reno, Nevada to Laguna Beach, California

Thomas had a great opportunity to advance his career, and I thought it would be exciting for us, so he moved to Lake Tahoe where he worked for a hotel and casino chain situated on the border of Nevada and California. I stayed in California so I could pull in an income and have a sense of financial security until I could find a job in Lake Tahoe, hopefully with the same company.

Thomas was supposed to be training to be the Vice President of Human Resources for the chain which included properties in Reno, Lake Tahoe, and Colorado. However, after two weeks on the job, his boss, the Vice President of Human Resources for the Northern Nevada Division, informed him that she was leaving to work for a competitor. We excitedly believed luck was on our side and that Thomas would get her job. Our excitement didn't last long. Instead of promoting him to the Vice President job as they promised, they promoted the Vice President of Human Resources for the Southern Nevada Division to a newly created position which consolidated all of the Nevada properties under a single Vice President of Human Resources. We were disappointed, as Thomas had taken a 20% pay cut to move to Reno for this opportunity.

We thought things might get better so we agreed he would stay in Reno. Within three months, I found a job working in Reno as the Director of Administration for the General Manager. Thomas was offered and accepted the position of Director of Human Resources for the chain with a modest increase in pay. We rented a house in Incline Village, and Thomas commuted around the east side of Lake Tahoe to work. I commuted up and over the mountain pass to Reno. In reality, it was a nightmare.

Thomas worked rotating shifts, mainly daytime hours, but once a week he worked a night shift and then a graveyard shift so he could meet the entire management team. He was also on call 24 hours a day, 7 days a week for any incident that happened at the chain, including bomb threats, arrests of the employees while on duty, etc.

As part of his job, we were expected to be available to host dignitaries and high rollers. We spent Christmas and New Year's Eve dining and dancing with elderly, wealthy men and women. We had season ski passes at Heavenly Valley, courtesy of Thomas' employer, but we were so busy working, there was no free time to use them. We both became frustrated. Our first winter in Lake Tahoe, from October through February, they received enough snow to fill the lake to its normal level in less than one year! Consequently, I was forced many nights to drive home from Reno to our home in Incline Village in a blizzard over Mount Rose Pass. I got to know Mount Rose Pass so well that the semi-trucks would follow close behind me and I would lead the parade of trucks up and over this dangerous pass.

We had taken a pay cut and moved to Nevada so we could enjoy our lives rather than waiting until retirement, but this wasn't the case. Thomas usually worked on Saturday, so when Sunday rolled around, we were too exhausted to do anything. After three months and many nights talking about the mistake we made in moving, we decided to return to Southern California, make decent wages again, and retire early.

Marriage Challenges

I was fortunate to return to my old job at the law firm since my managing partner had not found anyone to replace me. I returned to California and Thomas remained in Nevada for six months until he landed a job in Santa Ana, California with a rapidly growing high-tech distribution company. Once he got back, we bought a beautiful home in Laguna Beach.

Again, life was good, but it was also hectic. Working long hours added stress for both of us, and Thomas didn't manage the stress well. He began taking out his unhappiness on me. Because I knew it was stress related, I didn't think too much of it and tried to let things roll off my back. I had

Working long hours added stress for both of us, and Thomas didn't manage the stress well. He began taking out his unhappiness on me.

been mentally abused most of my life, so his words seemed like a normal way to live.

This continued for several years until I was asked to open my law firm's new Dallas office. I was working as their office administrator, opening new offices, hiring lawyers for multiple locations, and managing our annual partner retreat. I jumped on the opportunity and, in Dallas, was surrounded by people who were uplifting and appreciative of my work. My role was to manage the office and travel to Dallas every other week over the course of several months. It was a wonderful feeling to go to my hotel room each night and not hear criticism. I began to recognize a difference in how I felt when I was home in Laguna Beach versus when I was in Dallas with the uplifting attorneys and staff.

Thomas and I had wonderful friends in San Diego, and we would visit them at least once a month. My girlfriend was from Iowa and one weekend she asked me to visit Iowa with her. She and her husband were building a house on a lake and she wanted me to see it. So off we went for four days to the middle of corn fields. On our trip home, we had a layover in Chicago. Walking to the gate for the second leg of our flight, I passed a bookstore and a book in the front window caught my eye. It was about verbal abuse. As I stared at it, something told me to purchase it, so I did. I read a good portion of it on the way home and cried the entire time, realizing that Thomas was verbally abusive to me, and that I allowed his behavior because I thought it was normal. I began to understand that, during my lifetime, I had previously learned to overcompensate for people I loved because I was terrified of being abandoned. With this revelation, I knew it was time for a change.

Having experienced positivity in my life when I was with my friends in Dallas, I knew I didn't want to live in an abusive relationship with

Thomas any longer. One day after work, I confronted him, telling him I was drawing my line in the sand and would not take his verbal abuse any longer. Of course, he denied it was abuse, so I gave him the book and asked him to read it. Then I moved to the downstairs bedroom to give both of us some space.

This was an eye opener for Thomas, even though he didn't want to admit he had a problem. He quickly learned that he was a "poster child" for dishing out verbal abuse. Our relationship changed after that. Even though he became cognizant of the verbal abuse and tried to stem it, I had changed, and I felt our relationship starting to unravel. We were sleeping together but we were no longer sexually intimate. This continued for months as I emotionally drifted away. Not having sex didn't bother me at all, but it bothered Thomas. He was depressed and unhappy with our sex life, or lack thereof. We were the couple who was always hugging, holding hands, and making out in the back of friends' cars. They would jokingly call us rabbits because we couldn't keep our hands off each other.

Thomas started counseling with a psychologist with hopes of turning our relationship around. We also saw a marriage counselor together. After six months, I was unhappy and didn't see much change. I desperately needed some alone time to think things through. I asked Thomas to get an apartment and move out, and he reluctantly agreed. We continued seeing one another while we were separated, going to movies, the beach, or Thomas would help me with home or car repairs. Sometimes he would sleep over and we would cuddle, but no sex.

This continued for about three months. Then we decided to take a ski trip to Beaver Creek, Colorado. We both had a wonderful time, but I wasn't ready to resume a sexual relationship. Again, we slept in the same bed, which wasn't wise, but I had no sexual desire for him. He was still working through the verbal abuse issue, and he had a couple of episodes during our trip. I would shove my feelings down deep and keep going, but my self-esteem was on a downhill slide.

On our last night in Beaver Creek, we were celebrating the fact that we were getting along and that things were moving in the right direction. We enjoyed some wine and were sitting on the couch in front of a roaring fireplace. One thing led to another, and we made love. The next morning, Thomas thought everything was great until I told him I wanted a divorce. I explained that we had seen counselors on our own and together, but nothing was working to draw us closer. He was shattered, in shock, and devastated because he was working hard to be a good husband and patch up our marriage.

Unbeknownst to me, something inside Thomas snapped.

CHAPTER 16

Snapped

bout three months after we got back from Colorado, I invited Thomas over for dinner on a Friday night and extended the invitation for him to spend the night. I wanted to see whether there was hope to salvage the marriage or if I wanted to leave it. The answer would be made perfectly clear before the evening was over.

When Thomas snapped, he was unbalanced and his love for me became more of an obsession. Before he came for dinner, his plan was to drug me and have sex with me. He was incredibly desperate, and much sicker, mentally and emotionally, that even he realized. Thomas made us drinks before dinner (he slipped a rape drug into my drink), and I became extremely disoriented and went to bed. Thomas silently slipped into bed and, with a washcloth soaked in ether, he gently placed the washcloth on the pillow next to my head. A moment later, something spoke to him, asking what he was doing. He came to his senses and reached for the washcloth, but as he did, I woke up and asked him what I was smelling. Somehow, I knew Thomas was up to something strange even though I was asleep.[19]

When I heard him turn on the television in the other room, I somehow found the strength, slipped out of bed, and went into the bathroom to search his bag. What I found frightened me, but I kept calm. I grabbed the small bottle and poured some of the liquid from his bottle into one of my containers, making sure the lids were on tightly. Then I slid his bottle back into his bag, placed my bottle into a drawer, and returned to bed. When I woke up the next morning, Thomas was gone.

It was a Saturday and I wanted to speak to someone about what happened the night before. Even though I didn't have to work, I went into the office and called one of my partners, asking him to come to the office to speak with me about something personal. As I began to tell him about what had transpired the night before, I started to sob. I carefully removed the small bottle from my purse, opened it, and asked him to smell it. He took one whiff and was jolted by its stench. Without hesitation, he said it smelled like Ether and told me about a lab the firm used to test chemicals and other materials for ongoing cases going to trial. With that information, I went home. I couldn't take the bottle to the lab until Monday morning, so Sunday was spent in a shocked daze with non-stop crying. I still loved this man, yet I could not understand his actions.

On Monday morning, I went straight to the lab and gave the bottle to a lab technician, who said it would take a couple of days for the results.

After arriving at the police station, I sat in the car for what seemed an eternity. I was about to turn in my husband for attempted rape and give them the bottle of Ether as evidence.

While I waited, I spoke with my best friend and tried to figure out what to do. I knew Thomas needed serious help, and I did not believe he had the inclination to get the amount of help that was vital to his well-being.

On Wednesday morning, the lab called and said it was a strong level of Ether. I sat in my office and cried uncontrollably, making the decision to go to the Laguna Police Department. After arriving, I sat in the car for what seemed an eternity. I was about to turn in my husband for attempted rape and give them the bottle of Ether as evidence. How could I get the words out to tell the police, and did I really want to press charges? I sat with the Lord and prayed, and the next instant, I got out of my car, entered the police station, and asked to speak to an officer.

As I sat in the police department, I was living a total nightmare. I spoke with two plain clothes officers, recounting every detail of what happened between my estranged husband and me. They listened with great interest and, when I was finished telling my story, they asked if I would wear a wire and get him to admit what he had done. They explained that, unless I could get him to admit his actions while being recorded, it would be a "he said, she said" situation. I answered, "Yes." The Lord was working through my voice to answer because I didn't have the courage or strength to speak. But I had to help Thomas.

Still in the police department, I made a phone call to Thomas at work, with the two officers listening in, asking him point blank whether he tried to drug me the previous Friday night. I asked, "Did you even realize you could have killed me?" He was shocked and stuttered a bit on the phone, asking if he could talk with me in person later that evening. I agreed and asked him to come to the house. Before Thomas arrived, the officers planted a wire on me and sat in a car about two blocks away. I was beyond thinking that all hope was gone, feeling empty and numb inside.

When Thomas arrived, I was shaking when I answered the door. I had been crying off and on for days and it took everything in me not to blow his confession. So, when he came inside, I didn't let him sit down before I asked, "Did you try to drug me and have sex with me last Friday night?" He started to weep and said, "I have no idea what was wrong with me but, yes, I tried to drug you with the plan of raping you, but I couldn't go through with it. I'm going to get help, I promise. I'm on my way to see a therapist when I leave here." As Thomas was driving to his appointment, the police pulled him over, arrested him, and took him to jail.

Next to giving up my child, turning Thomas into the police was the second hardest thing I had ever done. I still loved my husband, but he needed help. I called one of our couple friends and told them I didn't want to live any longer. They came over to be with me and my girlfriend spent the night, making sure I was okay. We talked all night and we cried, talked, and cried. It was like we both lost a loved one because she and her husband also loved Thomas, as, deep down, he was a good person.

Arrested

The evening was not only miserable for me. Following are Thomas' words about his experience.

> *"I began driving south on the Pacific Coast Highway toward my psychologist's office. After about five miles, I heard a siren and saw red lights in my rearview mirror. I was pulled over by a Laguna Beach Police car. I knew I wasn't in a good frame of mind, so I thought perhaps I was weaving or speeding.*
>
> *"The officer asked for my license and then asked me to step out of the car. He then asked me to sit on the curb while he returned to his car, which I thought was odd. A few minutes later an unmarked car pulled up and a man in a suit got out and approached me. He gave his name and said he was a detective with the Laguna Beach Police Department. He asked my name and if I had any weapons on me or in my car. I shook my head and replied no, explaining that I didn't own any weapons. He then asked if they could search my car for weapons. At this point I thought this was really weird, but I told him okay. He proceeded to search the interior of my car and the trunk and found nothing except my briefcase and laptop computer.*

"The detective asked if I knew why I had been pulled over. Naturally, I was extremely perplexed at this point and needless to say, I was clueless. He told me that my wife had filed a complaint against me for attempted rape. My gut sank. I was thunderstruck. I could not believe that Vicky had turned me into the police. After our discussion, my tearful plea for forgiveness, my confessing, plus I was on my way to my psychologist to get help!

"The next thing I knew, I was cuffed and put in the back of the patrol car and taken to the Laguna Beach Police Department. I was read the Miranda rights, officially arrested, photographed, and fingerprinted. The police detective asked if I had any statement to make and I remained silent. He kept trying to get me to talk, but I said I had nothing to say, and that I had talked to my wife earlier in the evening.

"I spent the night in a holding cell at the police department because it was too late to transport me to the county jail. In the morning, I was transported to the county jail in Santa Ana and again photographed, fingerprinted, and processed. I was given an orange jumpsuit and slip-on sneakers to wear. On one hand, everything happened so fast I had no time to process what was happening; yet on the other hand, I had a horrible feeling in my gut.

"It took an entire day to be fully processed. I was in a group with thirty others, and they kept moving us from one barred room to another. My fellow prisoners called it making the rounds. The guards were absolutely horrible. They did everything they could to belittle us, make us feel stupid, or goad us into some form of conflict. It was a horrific

nightmare! I remember thinking, 'What happened to being innocent until proven guilty!?' That evening, after a bologna sandwich dinner, we were told that the county prison farm was overcrowded, and they did not have beds for us. So, we were instructed to lie down on the concrete floor and sleep that way for the night. I was dumbfounded. This is the United States and people awaiting their day in court have to sleep on a concrete floor?

"At some point during the evening, one of the guards called my name. He told me that my attorney wanted to speak with me. I followed him to another room which had a row of cubicles with a glass partition running down the center. Seated across from me was Greg, a good friend I've known for years. Not only was he an attorney, but he was also Vicky's boss. To be honest, I have no recollection of how he came to be there. I think I may have called him when I was first arrested (my one phone call) and left him a message, or Vicky told him what happened.

"When I saw Greg, I broke down and started to cry. I asked Greg for help and to do anything and everything he could to get me out of jail as quickly as he could. Greg is a civil litigation attorney, not a criminal defense attorney, so he was not allowed to represent me. He said my bail had been set at $250,000 and that it would cost $25,000 to secure a bail bond. I begged him, saying if he would secure the bail bond, I would repay him as soon as I was released. He said he would and that he would check around for the name of a good criminal defense attorney.

"It was quite late on this Saturday evening, and I was led back to the cell with the thirty other men who were sleeping on the cold concrete floor. I lay down and tried to sleep but a cold floor, no pillow, no blanket, and a mind that was spinning at 500 mph meant that sleep was not going to happen for me that night.

"The next day I was informed that bail had been made and that I would be released later that day. Well, the hours came and went. By late afternoon, I was taken to another room where they said I should wait until they were ready to release me. Again, hours passed, and it was early evening before they returned my clothes and personal belongings. They also gave me a copy of a restraining order that Vicky had filed, prohibiting me from contacting her, and ordered me to keep a physical distance from her, her home and where she worked. I was finally released but my car was still impounded in Laguna Beach. Given how late it was, I decided to call a taxi and have them take me to my apartment. I was thrilled at the thought of being in my own bed.

"When I got to my apartment, I was shocked to find my door smashed in with police tape across it. When I walked in, I discovered my apartment was totally trashed; everything had been taken out of the drawers and cabinets and strewn throughout the apartment. It was like one of those scenes from a movie after a house has been searched. Lying smack dab in the middle of the kitchen table was a search warrant. For the life of me, I can't understand why they didn't use my apartment key, which they had, or contact the apartment manager for access to my apartment. Why smash down the front door? I was thoroughly exhausted from the night before, so I just cleaned everything off the bed, got under a blanket, and cried myself to sleep.

"The next morning, I was thankful to return to work. The morning went well and after lunch, when I walked into my office, I was surprised to be greeted by my boss and the company's director of security. The Laguna Beach Police Department had served a search warrant for my office, my laptop, and access to the company's email records. My office was searched while I was out for lunch. My laptop had been confiscated and their forensic IT team had been in discussions with the company's IT department.

"I was mortified to see that this event spilled into my place of work. I was also ashamed and embarrassed! I told them that I was in the midst of a complicated divorce and that Vicky had filed charges against me. My boss and the director of security told me they understood, but I didn't believe them. I was close to both of them, and they emitted an aura that was not in sync with what they said. This was truly an uncomfortable situation. They asked me if I wanted to go home but I declined and stayed on for the rest of the day. I had to stay busy to keep my mind occupied.

"That afternoon, Greg called and said he had gotten the name of a criminal defense attorney for me. He said he didn't know this attorney, but he was highly regarded by some of Greg's attorney friends. I thanked him for the referral and immediately called this attorney, Paul, to book an appointment.

"The following day I met Paul, and I had a good feeling about him. He told me that the charges against me were serious and, if I were convicted, a felony. He asked me to tell him what had happened, and I did. I told him that I did *not rape Vicky and that the entire event was like a dream. I can remember the events, but they were as if someone else was there. He asked me if I was seeing a psychologist or psychiatrist and I told him I had been seeing a psychologist regularly for the past year or more. He encouraged me to continue with my therapy. He asked if I wanted him to represent me and if so, his retainer was $25,000, plus additional costs if we went to trial. He said that a hearing had been set for the following week but, thankfully, I was not required to attend as he could represent me before the court. I agreed and told him that I had an appointment that evening with my psychologist. He suggested that I talk to my psychologist about attending an SLAA meeting, which he explained is an acronym for 'Sex and Love Addicts Anonymous.' It was an organization similar to Alcoholics Anonymous, and I had no idea this existed."*

Filing for Divorce Number Two

The morning after Thomas was arrested, I didn't go to work. I called the office and told them I was sick. And I was; I was physically and emotionally drained.

A friend came over who encouraged me to file a restraining order against Thomas. I was apprehensive about the idea, but she was determined I should get one. She grabbed her purse, held my hand, and we drove to the courthouse. Before we entered the building, I stopped and told her I could not do it. Even after everything that happened, I didn't believe Thomas would intentionally hurt me. He desperately needed help and he was finally being forced to get it. We got back in the car and returned to my house. Meanwhile, I had no idea the police had automatically issued one.

Later that afternoon, I filed for divorce. While I still loved Thomas, I could not forgive him for what he had done. I had to move on and so did he. The divorce lawyer had been practicing family law for many years and, after I told her the story, she said she had never heard of such a thing happening to a client.

Then I took a few days off work. This felt like a turning point in my life, and I needed quiet time to reflect on things. Memories from my past flooded my thoughts and got muddled with my current situation. Thoughts about my mother overrode everything, as my brain was determined to tie my relationship with my mother to current day events.

CHAPTER 17

Reflecting on Abuse

I sat with these thoughts and memories, determined to get a full picture of the relationship that had wounded and scarred my heart, both as a child and as an adult. Sitting with brokenness was one of the hardest things I've ever done, but I wanted to be free of the anger, resentment, and bitterness once and for all. Many of the memories that surfaced helped me understand who I am and why I am the way I am. There's a saying, "You have to feel to heal," and that's the road these quiet reflective days took me down.

How we are raised has a huge bearing on a myriad of things in our lives, especially relationships. So, I started working through my early days of childhood and realized I was raised in an environment of domestic violence, which was the reason for my emotional distress, anxiety, mental health issues, and poor self-esteem. That was also the reason I struggled with hopelessness, feeling unloved and worthless, and why anger fueled my tongue for so many years. I could see how my parents' relationship when I was a child influenced my insecurities, fears, and my relationship with my brother.

How we are raised has a huge bearing on a myriad of things in our lives, especially relationships.

I remembered how my mother was domineering and controlling, how she needed to be the center of attention. I recalled how she was not sensitive to my needs. She was not affectionate, nor did she offer encouragement or acknowledgement for a job well done. I thought about the ridiculing and teasing, the verbal abuse, and how my mother treated me. The comment that stayed with me the longest is, "You're fat and always will be." I haven't been fat for most of my adult life, yet when I look in the mirror, I see a fat woman. I wondered if I would ever be able to work through the damage caused from being abused as an overweight child.

There was the abandonment I felt when she forced me to give my baby up for adoption. Feeling alone and isolated is like being on a deserted island with dark clouds rolling in and no way to get back to that wonderful place of being loved and accepted. How had the abandonment from being left alone in the maternity home affected every relationship after that? How had it impacted my self-worth and sense of value?

I also realized I had been surrounded by controlling and abusive people most of my life. In a bizarre way, it was so familiar that it seemed normal. My comfort zone was found in constant abuse from my mother, the lawyers I worked with each day, and my husband, and I took it all in stride.

I am convinced that, unless there is an ah-ha moment or a traumatic event that makes us ask questions, abuse can last a lifetime. The pain and anguish from my past were resurfacing with the trauma regarding Thomas, who had been verbally abusing me for years. However, his attempt to drug me so I could be raped was the last straw. I realized there was a better way to live, and I wanted a different life for Vicky Berry.

Many of us go through life not having a clue that we are victims of abuse. Psychological abuse can be hidden in many ways, so much so that the damage hides in the crevasses of our minds, which can take years to be freed so the healing can begin. In some cases, the damage is never healed. I was a victim of abuse, yet I had no clue it had been happening. Did I have an invisible blinking neon sign that read, *abuse me*, that only abusers could see? Like a moth to a light?

Once a perpetrator is attached to a relationship, whether it's in a family, the work environment, or a romantic relationship, these abusers attempt to tear down the qualities and success that drew them there to begin with. Far too many people think those who are in an abusive relationship are weak. This may well be the end result, but in reality, it doesn't start that way.

Victims of psychological abuse are most often the kind of people you wouldn't think would be vulnerable to such a thing. Strength and success are what attracts abusive narcissists and psychopaths to them. Psychological abuse starts with something small, such as a partner who criticizes for something unexpected. This goes against how they started out when they were in the romancing stage of the relationship, so it's often brushed off as an out-of-character moment. However, these moments incrementally become more frequent, yet, at the same time and at a slow pace, go unnoticed.

Some who engage in psychological abuse of their partners, colleagues, friends, or family are often narcissistic and believe they are, in some way, superior in order to feed what they are lacking in their life. There are others who have a need that must be filled in order to have some sense of control, and that need supersedes all else.

I thought about Dan and how we lost everything we owned because he was financially irresponsible. But that wasn't what broke my heart. The emotional abuse of his abandonment caused me to believe everyone else was more important than me, and he chose others because he thought they needed him more than I did. The rejection and abandonment I felt from him left me wondering if I was loveable.

I reflected on how grateful I was to have my father. He balanced things out so that I never saw my mother's abuse as such; I just saw her as a controlling woman. I thought about having to give up my baby, and how hearing of Paul's marriage three years later shattered my heart. I had lived with a false hope that things with us would work out and I would wake up from the horrible nightmare I was living in.

And then, I remembered that special day by the sea when my mother and I started over and was thankful we had those moments. I did not have long to spend with her after we started over because, a little over two years later, she got sick with cancer, and she died three months after that. But she was able to see me marry Thomas, and we spent many good times together as happy mother and daughter. She finally connected with me. Before she died, lying in her hospital bed, she said, "I'm so glad we are finally close. You are going to be fine after I am gone. I'm not worried about you. You will continue to make Thomas a good wife and do anything you want to do in your life. I am so proud of you and the woman you have become."

The truth of those horrible times of my childhood molestations was revealed during a painful session with my therapist as we discussed my childhood. The secret was locked in the inner sanctum of my mind where I buried those horrific episodes. Digging in the darkest holes of my consciousness brought this horrible experience into the light where I could begin to deal with reality and start the long road to forgiveness. My secret was hidden away for decades, and I never told my parents, friends, or anyone else that my innocence was taken when I was ten. The hate for these boys was buried so deep within me, it felt like I had dug for centuries to create a hole deep enough to bury the hatred and hurt.

There's a saying, "What doesn't break you will make you." I believe that, to some degree, I became more determined and stronger, and ended up with a successful career. But no matter how strong or successful I appeared, deep inside were unresolved issues that held me back from being content and at peace with life and myself. I had to sit with each of these issues and work through them so I could move forward.

"I, even I, am he who blots out your transgressions,
for my own sake, and remembers your sins no more."
Isaiah 43:25

CHAPTER 18

Letting Go

decided it was time to get on with life and figure out who Vicky Berry wanted to become. Enough of letting the past dictate how I felt and what I did. That black cloud constantly hovering over my head had to go away; I needed a fresh start. I knew it would be a new chapter, and that's what I wanted.

In the process, a couple of Bible verses really helped me.

> *"But one thing I do, forgetting those things which are behind*
> *and reaching forward to those things which are ahead.*
> *I press toward the goal for the prize of the upward*
> *call of God in Christ Jesus."*
> Philippians 3:12

> *"Let all bitterness and wrath and anger and clamor and slander*
> *be put away from you, along with all malice.*
> *Be kind to one another, tenderhearted, forgiving one another,*
> *as God in Christ forgave you."*
> Ephesians 4:31-32

The weeks that followed found me in a daze. I tried to think positive thoughts and I tried reading Bible passages, but I would no sooner start than I would give up. It was too easy to do nothing. Every day, I was on autopilot mode: wake up, go to work, come home, have dinner, go to bed. Repeat. I even worked on the weekends to keep from facing an empty house. I wanted to change, but I was in a wicked rut.

Through a mutual friend, I learned that Thomas was out of jail and going to counseling several times a week. He was also dedicated to attending a recovery group at church. This news lifted my spirit because I wanted him to get help and be well. After everything he put me through, I wasn't angry with him.

To keep me moving forward, I talked to one of my best friends from Florida almost every day. I was also seeing a Christian counselor to try to navigate through what happened to our marriage and to me. I refused to brush anything under the rug ever again. I had learned the hard way that anything shoved under a rug will find its way out eventually, so I chose to deal with everything sooner than later. Before I could move on, I finally realized I had to heal and become whole again.

It was then I understood that I was special to the Lord, and I didn't need anyone else in my life to make me whole. I began to feel loved and comfortable with who He created me to be. I was in His hands; that is when my healing began.

For months, I didn't socialize. Those weeks were filled with work, church, boot camp exercises, and counseling sessions, which was what I needed on my journey to being healed. I spent a great deal of time alone with my Lord who helped me not only to draw closer to Him at every level, but to begin to love the person I was becoming. Thomas agreed to give me his part of the house in the divorce proceedings, and I did what I could to make it my sanctuary. I changed several things in the bedroom so that memories would not haunt me as I slept there. I changed other parts of the house to make it mine. Thomas never wanted hardwood floors, so the first thing I did was to have the carpeting ripped out and hardwoods installed. I also purchased a movie-style popcorn maker, something Thomas never wanted, and when it arrived, I ate five helpings of popcorn the first night.

While the nights were lonely, I learned to sleep in the middle of the bed. I also continued to have phone conversations with my best friend in Florida. On the weekends, I would go to Laguna and run by the ocean and then stop by Starbucks for my favorite coffee. I spent long days at work and poured myself into my career, working at a prestigious law firm as their Director of Professional Development and Training. This firm had fourteen offices, including three in Europe. I've always been an overachiever but during this time of my life, I put my overachieving to work. I spent a great deal of time on the road between offices. It was great medicine to use my talents in such a positive way. I started every morning by asking the Lord to help me make a difference in one person's life. I knew it would make my day perfect if I could accomplish that one request.

Throughout this time, the prosecutor's office and the police department kept calling, trying to coerce me into filing formal charges against Thomas. I refused. What was the point? He was getting help and moving on. Through the Lord's grace, I had already forgiven him.

Returning to the Dating Scene

After six months, the divorce was final. After a year, I was ready to start dating. I didn't want to be alone for the rest of my life, even though mentally I was prepared to do so. I also wasn't willing to rush into anything just for the sake of having a man in my life. Some friends tried setting me up with guys, but I couldn't click with them. I started going out socially with my girlfriends which helped me on my healing journey. Once in a while, I would meet a guy, but again, nothing clicked.

I was frequently lonely but, with the Lord, I was never alone and never felt abandoned. We spent a lot of time together and He showed me how

I was frequently lonely but, with the Lord, I was never alone and never felt abandoned.

much He loves me and that He would never leave me or forsake me. I never felt more confident and comfortable with myself.

One day I decided to try online dating. I met a divorced gentleman who owned his own business, had a young daughter, and had similar likes. We dated for a few months, but the bells and whistles never went off. After six months, we knew we were not meant to be. After that, it was almost comical because I went on a lot of first dates to a local restaurant on the water in Laguna. I strategically picked this spot because it was a mile from my house, and I could go home early if I didn't like the guy. The valet guys greeted me by name and asked for a thumbs up or down when I left. I met television and movie producers, writers, a pharmaceutical owner, a script writer, stockbrokers, lawyers, doctors, and the list goes on. It was a lonely existence, so I held onto my Lord with all my might, trusting Him that the right guy would come along some day.

Four and a half years after the divorce, I met a nice gentleman, or so I thought, from an online dating site. We met for lunch and, although things seemed okay, little did I realize that he was a con artist. After about three months of dating, I began to notice little discrepancies in his stories, which should have been a red flag. I didn't worry at that point because we got along so well. He took me everywhere and treated me nicely, so I chose not to notice his little lies. In reality, I should have run in the opposite direction. He told me he was divorced and had two children. After six months of seeing each other, he became obsessed about seeing me every day and wanted to move in with me. (Does *obsessed* ring a bell?)

One afternoon, I received a call from someone I knew at the Irvine Police Department. He asked, "Do you know that the guy you are seeing is married and has been arrested for stalking his ex-girlfriend?" I was shocked. How could I allow myself to be taken in by someone like this man? Was I that desperate? Why didn't I listen to my instincts? The alarm bells were finally ringing loudly enough for me to pay attention and get away from him.

That evening I confronted him about his marriage and stalking his ex-girlfriend. He adamantly denied both things and told me how much he loved me and wanted us to move in together. I carefully explained that I didn't want a relationship with him any longer. I asked him to leave and, after half an hour of begging and pleading his case, he left. The following day, the office receptionist called me to the front desk to pick up a letter addressed to me. I found it unnerving that a handwritten letter, dropped off by someone, was left without the person asking to see me. I returned to my office and, when I opened it, the contents scared me. Immediately I called my best friend in Florida, and we talked at length about what my next move should be. I decided to send him a short, to-the-point email asking him to never contact me again, in any manner, emphasizing that our relationship was over and I no longer wanted to see him.

There were numerous phone calls from him after that, which I refused to answer. There was also a barrage of emails I refused to respond to. About two weeks later, at two o'clock in the morning, I heard banging at my front door. I was mortified. I had my house alarm on, but I was still scared that he was there to hurt me. I called 911 and they arrived minutes later. I explained everything to them, who he was, and what had been going on the past two weeks. They advised me to get a restraining order against him, which I proceeded to do. Another week went by and I didn't hear from him, but I knew not to let my guard down. Then another email message arrived. This time I responded and told him that if he were to continue contacting me, I would have him arrested for stalking. Once again, I asked him to refrain from contacting me.

I did not hear from him again.

Just as the dust was settling from this ordeal, Thomas and I began seeing each other again.

CHAPTER 19

A New Chapter

As I was trying to shake my head over what happened with this guy, I knew there was still work to be done on me. Meanwhile, as the weeks went by, a lot was happening with Thomas. The following is his account of what was going on.

"Some time went by, and I finally had a meeting with my attorney. He said he had gone to court on my behalf to enter a plea of not guilty. However, before it got to that point, the judge sent the case back to the District Attorney's office for further investigation and evidence. The District Attorney's office then sent my case file back to the Laguna Beach Police Department for follow-up. So, at that point in time, I had not been formally charged with a crime. Regardless, it still weighed heavily on me, and I was distressed.

"Several months passed and I finally received a call from my attorney. He was truly an amazing lawyer. He explained that he had tried to follow up with the status of my case through some inside sources, as he did not want to call attention or raise any red flags about my case. To his and my astonishment, the case file had gone missing. No one knew what happened; the DA's office may have lost it; it may have gotten lost in transit to the Laguna Beach Police Department; or it may have been lost or misfiled by the Laguna Beach Police. The bottom line: there was no case pending against me! It was difficult to know whether I should celebrate or live with the unknown hanging over me. What if one day the file magically reappeared?

"Regardless, my attorney advised me to continue with my counseling and SLAA (Sex and Love Addict Anonymous) meetings and to go about my normal daily affairs. He did forewarn me that it was possible that my case file could resurface at any time and the investigation would continue. Luckily, nothing came of it and, after five years, it ended when the statute of limitation passed. In thinking back on this strange set of circumstances, I am positive God had a hand in it.

"On the day of what would have been our nineteenth wedding anniversary, I was in my office when I received a call from the front lobby receptionist. She said that there was a gentleman in the lobby who wished to see me. As I approached the lobby waiting area, I could see a couple of individuals I didn't recognize. As I got closer, one of them approached me. I introduced myself and, as I held my hand out to shake his hand, he placed an envelope in my extended hand. Wow, how devious! He said I had been served legal documents. I had no idea what to think so I studied the envelope as I walked back to my office. I opened the envelope thinking it was some legal matter related to my employment. But no. It was a petition and summons for the dissolution of my marriage to Vicky. My heart dropped.

"I was, of course, stunned and shocked, yet in a crazy way, not surprised. It hurt more because it was our anniversary day. I highly suspected that Vicky's divorce attorney orchestrated this to inflict deep emotional pain; and without a doubt, she did a good job of that!

"I didn't see the necessity of hiring a divorce attorney, as the only thing we had to agree on was the division of our property and belongings. I agreed to release my interest in our home in exchange for retaining my stock options and retirement plans. We put together a list of our belongings and mutually agreed to their division. There was little debt and nothing significant that we could not agree upon, so thankfully the divorce went smoothly and rapidly.

"I continued seeing my therapist and attending SLAA meetings for the next two years. I attended church most Sundays and prayed for forgiveness and a new start on life. I thanked the Lord every day that I did not have to go to court for my transgressions. My life surely would be a lot different had I gone through the legal system. It took me a little over two years through therapy and SLAA to finally begin to understand what had happened and to forgive myself.

"During this period, I didn't have much of a life outside of work and church. I would get together with one of my best friends on Friday evenings for a couple of beers at the Tap Room Bar and Restaurant, but that was about it.

"I joined the Car Ministry at church. I love cars and as soon as I heard about this ministry, I knew it was a calling from God. The Car Ministry solicited donations of used cars from

103

church members and the general public. We would then inspect the donated car and either sell it to a wholesaler or scrap yard or keep it. If we found a car that we thought was salvageable and sellable, we would refurbish it (tires, brakes, tune-up, minor mechanical and cosmetic repairs, etc.). The refurbished cars were then advertised and sold to the general public or given to a church member who needed transportation. All proceeds were given to the church. I was pleasantly surprised that the church was doing this, and it was amazing being a part of it. It was truly a wonderful experience.

"I didn't think about dating until I felt I had turned the page to my new life. Like many middle-aged singles who work long hours and don't hang out at bars, it was difficult to meet single women. So, I turned to on-line dating services to seek female companionship. I casually dated quite a few women but only for a short time (usually one or two dates) until I got to know them. It was difficult, as I was always comparing them to Vicky, and I always found something I didn't like about them. In a crazy way, it was as though I was intentionally seeking a reason not to go past two dates.

"After about a year of casual dating, I met an attractive divorced woman, about my age, who had a nine-year-old son. She was born and raised in Colombia, South America. Her family was wealthy (and no…. not drug related) and she grew up with a personal maid and servants in the home. She eventually met and married a young doctor and they moved to the U.S. Again, she was well taken care of and lived in a huge house in the Midwest. Her husband fell in love with one of the nurses that worked with him and so they divorced. She moved to California and met another doctor (a radiologist) and they soon married and had a son. She was a stay-at-home mom and enjoyed it. Again, a divorce ensued over another woman, and she was left with the son, a condominium, and a sizeable alimony payment. We dated for a little over a year. I really liked her, but as time went by, I realized the relationship was missing something. She had never worked, and she made it clear that she did not want to work for a living. If I married her, I am sure we would have gotten by, but I certainly could not provide for her in the manner which she was accustomed to with her previous doctor husbands. The more I thought about that, it bothered me.

"She began to drop some not so subtle hints about getting married and I still had some doubts that the relationship would work in the long run. She had moved a lot of her clothes and personal things into my condominium and would stay with me whenever she did not have her son. I was okay with that, but still had the comfort of knowing she had her home to go to. One day I returned home to find she had packed all of her belongings and moved out. She left a note saying she did not think I would marry her, and she was wasting her time with me. Period - end of story - end of the relationship. She never spoke to me again. I was upset but, at the same time, angry that she did not have the decency to tell me to my face and discuss her concerns with me. As it turned out, it was all for the best.

"So, I continued on day-by-day and seemed fine not having a woman in my life. I often thought about Vicky. Vicky and I met as friends and got married as friends. We remained friends during and after the divorce. We didn't see each other *much after our divorce but she would occasionally call me for advice when her car was having trouble, or something wasn't working at the house. I really didn't mind going over to her house (our former home) to perform some minor repairs or diagnose a problem. I knew she had been a prolific dater after our divorce and was in a serious relationship with one gentleman.*

"One day at work I received a call from her. She said that the pool sweep in her swimming pool was not working. She asked if I could stop by sometime and take a look at it. I said I could come over the next Saturday if that would work for her, and she replied that would be fine. That Saturday I arrived at the house and examined the pool sweep; it was shot, and she would need to buy a new one. As we talked, she asked me how things were going with my girlfriend. I told her that we had broken up and had gone our separate ways. She didn't look surprised, as she knew things had not been going well between us. I asked her how she and her boyfriend were doing. She said that she too had just broken off their relationship because she discovered he was an embezzler, a stalker, and much more. With that, I mentioned that I had planned to go to the movies that night and didn't like going alone (which was a true statement) and asked if she would like to accompany me. She said that it sounded nice, and she would. We went to the movies and then spent most of the night talking about our lives and our futures. It was as if we had never been apart, though both of us had changed dramatically, for the better. With a new beginning, we began to officially date and have never been apart since.

"We sure did take our time. There was no way either one of us wanted to make another mistake. One night, after about a year of dating and getting to know each other again, Vicky blurted out she was ready to take the next step and wanted to see how we would do living together. So, she asked me if I would like to move in with her. Of course, I jumped at the chance and said yes. And with that, I moved in and leased out my house. During the following year we had our ups and downs as all couples do, but it was great to be together again. Reunited and it felt so good- just like that song says. We worked, traveled, socialized with friends, and most of all, we were always there for each other. Funny really, I had forgotten all the little things she did that made me so happy during our previous marriage.

"After living together for a year, I thought the time was finally right to ask her to remarry me, even though she never even hinted at it. We planned a trip to Paris, which was our favorite get-away destination, and I thought it would be a wonderful and romantic place to propose. I had gone to her favorite jeweler and purchased a beautiful diamond, and had it set in a temporary ring until she could pick out a setting she really wanted. We flew to Paris and had a fabulous week there. One night we took the elevator up to the top of the Eiffel Tower to view the magnificent city lights all around us. When we were at the top, I slipped my hand into my pocket and brought out the ring box. I got on my knee in front of her and told her I loved her and didn't ever want to be apart from her again. 'Will you marry me?' She gave me a big hug and replied with a quick – no.

"Vicky felt she wasn't ready. I was shocked and disappointed beyond belief! I loved her so much, and I thought she loved

me equally. We had dinner later at a little restaurant on the island of Isle Saint Louis in the middle of the Seine River. This was one of our favorite spots in Paris. Over dinner she explained that she indeed loved me, but she was not quite ready for marriage. Perhaps with a bit more time. Vicky reiterated that she loved me but felt she needed some more time to heal and feel 100 percent certain that we had both changed for the good of the relationship. Although I felt somewhat hurt, I knew well enough not to push or urge her and to give her the time she needed.

"We returned home and I kept the ring in a safe place just in case she changed her mind. We continued to live together and carried on in our day-to-day living.

"About nine months after our return from Paris, she had a birthday coming up and I planned a trip for us to the island of St. Lucia in the Caribbean. Neither of us had been there before so this was something we were looking forward to. It was nothing short of gorgeous on this island. Vicky and I had a wonderful time snorkeling in the clear ocean waters, floating on tubes in our private swimming pool, enjoying the magnificent views of the Piton mountains jutting up from the sea outside our villa window, having wonderful dinners in town and at our resort, and just relaxing and enjoying each other. On her birthday, we went into town for dinner. When we returned, we started to head toward the bar. As we approached, I grabbed her arm and turned her toward me. I again pulled the ring from my pocket and asked if she would marry me. I had to try again and, thankfully, I did because this time, she replied with a fast…. yes!"

Remarriage

Thomas and I began dating again and after six months I asked him to move back "home." I was determined to witness and feel the miracle that the Lord had done in Thomas's life. I saw the change in him when we were dating again but I wanted to live with him 24/7 to make sure that the old Thomas did not show up again. After several months of living together we made a trip to St. Lucia for my birthday. Thomas took out a beautiful diamond ring and asked me to marry him for the second time (the first time he asked was in Paris) and I said "yes." Thomas and I were married one year later on April 6th (the same date as our first wedding).

We had two ceremonies in our two favorite places in the world, Paris and South Africa. We had a religious ceremony in Paris at the American Church on the banks of the Seine River which was attended by Thomas' best friend, who was his best man, and his girlfriend. I had my best girlfriend and her husband come, as she was the maid of honor. We could not have the civil (legal) part of the marriage in France because U.S. citizens needed to be a resident of France for a minimum of thirty days. So, we left our friends in Paris and flew to South Africa.

There are no residency requirements in South Africa and the U.S. recognizes marriages that take place in South Africa as legal. We were married beside a beautiful watering hole on the Leopard Hills Private Game Reserve. A minister from a local town performed the ceremony and we were serenaded by a group of local native singers and dancers. It was amazing! During the ceremony, we were carefully escorted and watched by one of the Game Rangers with his rifle, just in case one of the local lions decided to come for a drink of water and a snack! To this day, Thomas jokes about how we had a shot-gun wedding! It's always a great topic of conversation when we meet new people at social events.

Figure 9 Married in Paris

Figure 10 Married in South Africa

CHAPTER 20

Restored Hope

One day when we were on our deck in Big Bear, California, I told Thomas I was thinking about starting to look for my child again since I hadn't gotten anywhere in past attempts. He was supportive, but suggested I wait until he or she was at least seventeen, to let my child finish high school. I reluctantly agreed. Those two years went by quickly, and I was eager to begin the search.

I contacted the hospital where my child was born. Since it was a private adoption, there were no records except that a birth occurred. When I asked for a copy of my hospital records, they said since it was such a long time ago, they were in the archives, and it would take a few days before they would have the chance to look.

When I called back a week later, they had no record of me being in the hospital. According to the person I spoke to, they had lost a considerable number of patient records during that time, including mine. Needless to say, I had no real place to start and wondered whether it was worth pursuing, since I would

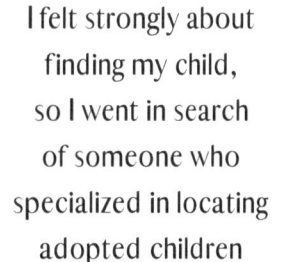

I felt strongly about finding my child, so I went in search of someone who specialized in locating adopted children

have to hire a private investigator. All I could think about was that my child was out there somewhere. What was his or her childhood like? Was college happening? Or worst of all, was my child still alive?

I felt strongly about finding my child, so I went in search of someone who specialized in locating adopted children. I found such a person in Oregon and, after a lengthy discussion, hired her. I only knew what day my child was born and in which hospital. But since the records were missing, she had to dig deep.

Several months after I hired my first private investigator, she had not made much progress. Finding my child was like finding a needle in a haystack. But she continued to follow up on leads in the general area where my child was born. After a year, she called with the sad news that she was ill and could no longer pursue the search. I was discouraged and wondered whether the Lord wanted me to proceed with finding my child.

It wasn't long afterward that Thomas and I visited my aunt Betty Lou in Hollywood. During our conversation, she asked if I had looked for my child and I told her I wasn't having any luck. She asked how old my son would be now, and I almost fainted! SON!?! What?! I had no idea she knew the gender of my child. She said my mother, father, and she knew but my mother didn't want me to know they knew. Auntie apologized for slipping with the news and said she should have told me earlier but didn't want to betray my mom.

This news confirmed what I knew all along in my gut while carrying my child – I had a son. At the very least, I had a solid foundation to keep looking because I was beginning to feel that I should give up.

A couple of years went by before I could seek out another private investigator. After many months, he determined the name of the adoptive parents. Through the people I stayed with at the maternity home, the names of my child's parents were finally located, after a long search. What we didn't know was that the father worked in the oil industry and moved the family all over the world. So, when we thought we had made progress, he would come up with another loose end.

Shortly after, the private investigator informed me that my son had been located. I was overjoyed to know he was still alive and hopefully happy and in good health. I asked him not to tell me my child's name or address because I did not want the temptation of going there if he did not want to meet me.

First things first. I wrote a letter to my son outlining what had happened to him and why he was put up for adoption. I told him about myself and that I was overjoyed to learn he was alive. I made sure he knew that I did not know his name, nor did I know where he was living, because I wanted him to know I would not contact him under any circumstance. I explained that, if he did not want to meet me, I completely understood, but I hoped that one day he would. I left him my contact information and told him I would pray that someday we would meet. I finished the letter, and the private investigator hand delivered it to him the following week.

And then, there was absolute silence for three years.

This wasn't the first letter I had written to my child. I wrote a letter to my baby when I was at the maternity home waiting for my child to be born. One of the conditions of the adoption was that the adoptive parents had to give my letter to my child when he or she was old enough to understand he or she had been adopted. The adoptive parents kept their word to give him the letter and I later discovered he was in his early teens. You see his adoptive parents adopted another child (a boy) a few years after adopting my son. So, when the boys began asking questions about being adopted, the adoptive parents gave my child the letter I wrote when I was seventeen. My child had experienced a loving childhood and saw his adoptive parents as his real parents.

I tried each day to work through the pain of not having my son contact me, but I promised myself and the Lord that I would be happy knowing he was alive and well, and I left my child at the Lord's feet and I prayed for him each day. I watched while folks I worked with had babies and brought their children into work and introduced them to me. The hurt was sometimes unbearable, but I believed that someday I would meet him in heaven.

My professional development and training job kept me on the road. One Friday, I was walking through the Houston airport headed home after a long week with a challenging partner. After I checked in, I looked at my phone, browsing the numerous email messages in my inbox, when I noticed one particular message. In the subject line it read, "Hello, this is Michael, your son." I started weeping before I could even open the message. Several people in the airport asked if I was okay. Okay? Was I okay? Yes, Yes, Yes, Yes! I heard from my son for the first time since he was born!

I immediately called Thomas and forwarded the email message to him. I did not want to immediately respond because I was too emotional to string two sentences together. So, I got on the plane headed for home, thanking the Lord for this gift of finally hearing from my wonderful son! It occurred to me on the way home that his name is Michael! Somehow, I knew it was a boy when he was in my womb, and, before he was born, I was planning to name him either Michael or Christopher. In a bizarre turn of events, I found out that Michael's brother, who is also adopted, is named Christopher.

The next morning, I responded to Michael's email message. It was difficult not to sound *over the top* with my response. I wanted to get to know him. In his email, he told me about his adoptive parents and his engagement to Julie and he sent a picture of himself and Julie. I was floored because he looked just like me and his father...there was no mistake he was mine. I asked if we could continue conversing by email but asked if we might connect by phone sometime in the future. I sent him a picture of Thomas and me so he, too, could see me for the first time. We conversed by email for several months. It was wonderful getting to personally know him, even though it was in written form and sent through an impersonal server.

"Hope deferred makes the heart sick, but a longing fulfilled is a tree of life."
Proverbs 13:12

CHAPTER 21

Somewhere Over the Rainbow

The week before Valentine's Day in 2010, I received a voicemail at work from my son. When I listened to it, I sat at my desk and wept. It was the first time hearing my son's voice. I must have played the message fifty times before the shock wore off, and I realized he wanted to come to Laguna Beach from Las Vegas with his fiancé to meet me for the first time. The date would be Valentine's Day weekend. Of course, the answer was YES! I called to tell Thomas and he said he was checking the calendar! I said, "Why on earth would you do that? I don't care if the Pope is on the calendar, clear it because we get to meet Michael for the FIRST time!"

Not knowing what Michael or Julie liked to eat, I purchased several different appetizers. We planned to open a nice bottle of French champagne to celebrate this occasion I had waited for since I was seventeen years old. As it turned out, Michael and Julie hit a traffic jam on their way, so he called and said they would be late. I began to pace the floor. After pacing for quite some time, I decided to make some popcorn. Thomas just smiled and asked, "So why are you making popcorn when we have so many appetizers?" I answered, "I don't know," and he just laughed!

About an hour later, there was a knock at the door. When Thomas and I opened the door, there stood Michael (6'2") and Julie (6') and me (5'2"). I asked Michael if I could hug him, and he said yes. We hugged, and I cried for quite some time. The feeling when I took my son in my arms for the first time is simply indescribable. It was the happiest moment to finally hold my Michael. He was even more handsome in person and Julie was drop-dead gorgeous. Then Thomas hugged him, and I hugged Julie. We asked them to come in and we went upstairs to the patio overlooking the ocean.

As soon as we sat down, Julie asked, "Do I smell popcorn?" I laughed and answered, "Yes." She said, "Popcorn is one of Michael's favorite things in the world." I almost lost my breakfast! Thomas opened the champagne and we toasted to first meetings. As I headed to get the appetizers, Julie asked if she could help. She followed me downstairs, and I hugged her again and said, "I had a feeling you were the reason Michael finally contacted me."

She said, "I told Michael that I would support him no matter what he decided, but that he needed to let you know one way or the other." She continued, "He was afraid of what you would be like and whether things would go well. He has other friends who are adopted and meeting their birth parents didn't go well for any of them. Michael worried about how to explain to our children, when we have them, why they have three sets of grandparents and, of course, the dynamic between his adoptive parents and you and Thomas. He was extremely apprehensive, but he decided he wanted to meet the person who had chosen life for him."

As the day progressed, it seemed we had known each other all of Michael's life. He brought photo albums of his childhood. He told me of the many places his family moved. That evening, we took Michael and Julie to one of our favorite restaurants and, during dinner, Michael asked if Thomas and I would come to their wedding in July. I was on top of the world. He was 36 years old, and I would see him get married for the first time!

That evening we talked until midnight when Michael and Julie left for their hotel. The next morning, we took them for breakfast on the beach and the conversation kept going until it was time for them to leave. I packaged a lunch for them, including fresh popcorn, and walked them to the car. I held Michael for the longest time and told him that I loved him, and he was the best Valentine's present ever.

Figure 11 Meeting Michael the first time

Thomas and I went back into the house and recalled the weekend with our newly found son and soon to be daughter-in-law. We thanked our Lord for this gift and asked that He continue His work in our lives.

The following Tuesday, Michael called and said he had the upcoming weekend off work and asked if we were free. I was thrilled that he and

Julie wanted to see us again and, this time, they wanted to stay with us so we could spend as much time together as possible. I cannot describe how excited I was to see them again, so soon!

On the Thursday night before Michael and Julie were to arrive, I received a call from Michael's adoptive mother, Dixie. When I picked up the phone, she said, "Hi Vicky, this is Dixie, and I want to thank you for giving birth to my son." Through tears, I thanked her for raising such an amazing man, telling her that Michael would not be the wonderful man he is without her and Michael's father. We chatted for a few minutes and talked about traveling to Colorado to their home to meet them before the wedding in July.

Friday and Saturday with Michael and Julie flew by. I made lasagna for dinner, not knowing that was Michael's favorite meal. During dinner I went into the kitchen to get butter for the bread and, when I returned, Michael was talking about the music for the wedding. He said he really liked the song, *Somewhere over the Rainbow*. I dropped the butter dish on the floor and pieces of the plate and butter went flying everywhere.

As I told him the story of how I sang that song to him every day he was in my womb, I began to cry. That song gave me hope that I would someday find the pot of gold (him) at the end of the rainbow. We were like two peas in a pod.

> Michael was talking about the music for the wedding. He said he really liked the song, *Somewhere over the Rainbow.*

Michael wanted us to meet his adoptive parents before the wedding in July. So, Thomas and I few to Colorado Springs in early June to meet them in person. When Thomas and I arrived at his parents' home in Colorado, they greeted us with open arms.[20] Michael's father, Rick, hugged me, cried, and thanked me for bringing Michael into the world. Rick said that Michael was such a gift to them, and they were happy to have been given the opportunity to raise him. We had a delightful weekend, taking long hikes, having dinner in their home, and touring Colorado Springs. We saw Michael's high school and their old home where Michael was raised during his teenage years.

When we got on the airplane on Sunday to head home, Thomas and I thanked the Lord for such a good meeting with Michael's adoptive parents.

On July 8, Michael and Julie were married at the Garden of the Gods and, believe it or not, it snowed! We did, however, get to have the ceremony outside and, while it was chilly, I did not notice! I was so proud to be introduced to so many friends and family. My emotions were raw and I could not stop crying. Not only did I get to meet my Michael and Julie in February, but I was able to see them wed and meet all the special people in their lives.

As the evening wore on, over the loudspeakers I heard, *Somewhere over the Rainbow*. When I looked up, Michael was standing beside me, holding out his hand for me to dance. For the first time in my life, I danced with my son to the song I had sung to him over 36 years earlier. It was magical.

As I pondered the miraculous events that made that evening possible, I thought how proud my mother and father would have been of their grandson. Since the Lord helped me to unconditionally forgive my parents for abandoning me and forcing me to give up my son, I had no anger toward them. I had only unconditional love and a feeling of complete redemption.

Unconditional forgiveness is powerful. It heals your heart, your spirit, your body, and your soul.

"You, Lord, are forgiving and good,
abounding in love to all who call on you."
Psalm 86:5

Figure 12 Michael and Julie with me and Thomas

EPILOGUE

The Lord's unconditional forgiveness has slowly but surely removed the burden of the emotional anvil that weighed me down. Negative emotions that surfaced because of abandonment, abuse, betrayal, and so many other things, had to be dealt with and resolved. Offering unconditional forgiveness to those who caused the hurt gave me wings to soar high above the rainbow with Him. Through that process, I found contentment, peace, and blessings.

He has blessed me more than I could ask or imagine! Michael and I were reunited over twelve years ago, and it is still amazing how much alike we are! Thomas and I have been remarried for over a decade. We couldn't be happier and are still crazy in love with each other. Whenever I think about the tough times Thomas and I endured before our remarriage, I don't remember much.

We both retired 10 years ago on April 6 (our wedding date) and are currently living in a beautiful mountain home in Bigfork, Montana. We have once again become close with Thomas' two daughters from his previous marriage and my new-found son and his wife. We have three grandchildren, and I reunited with Steven, my precious brother.

After we moved to Montana, Steven had a heart attack. We drove non-stop to Oregon to be with him. When I walked into his hospital room, he was asleep, and I gently touched his cheek. When he awoke, big tears formed in his eyes, and he asked why I was there. I said, "I heard my brother was sick, so we came to be with him. He's the only brother I have on this earth." It was during that moment and the next couple of days we spent with him that we became the best of friends. I enjoyed becoming close again, talking about our Oregon Ducks, the grandkids, and the joy of discovering Steven find the Lord. Unfortunately, I have had to endure another loss in my life. My sweet and amazing Steven went to be with the Lord in December of 2022. I still grieve his passing but knowing he is with our Lord makes me smile.

Life brings each of us great challenges, but it is our faith in the Lord that gets us through those times. Without a doubt, the Lord has brought such immense joy, peace, and happiness to us. I pray each day for His love and forgiveness in our lives. Through Him we were able to unconditionally forgive each other, ourselves, and the many who hurt us over the years. I am totally at peace through our Lord's grace, unconditional forgiveness, and redemption. Amen!

"Even if my father and mother abandoned me, the Lord will take me in."
Psalm 27:10

ABOUT THE AUTHOR

A retired professional in the highly competitive legal field, Vicky Berry made an early statement around the legal world with a groundbreaking University that trained all the lawyers in her firm. Of course, there were many other accomplishments throughout a long and successful legal career. She started writing this book shortly after her retirement.

A bona fide world traveler, Vicky loves to visit and learn about other cultures and the people that reside in each one, attempting to spread the love of Christ. Whether in her two favorite settings of Africa and Paris or the stunning, storybook village in Northwestern Montana where she resides, Vicky loves to touch others with His love and compassion.

A staunch fan of her alma mater [Go Ducks!], and football in general the Lord has blessed her to find true love not once, but twice, with the same man. Yes, Vicky married her husband and best friend in 1985, then again in 2010, a love story chronicled in this book. They enjoy a relaxed and well-earned lifestyle in Montana's Rocky Mountains with their beloved miniature dachshunds, Chloe and Cooper.

For more, visit www.findingtheendoftherainbow.com.

Figure 13 Chloe and Cooper

NOTES

1   Dion, Celine. "You and I." *A New Day…Live in Las Vegas.* Written by Nova, Aldo, Duval, Jacques. Masterplan Studios, 2004.

2   It's hard to think that Ironwood, Michigan had the largest ski jumping hill in the U.S. at that time. Although not opened until 1969, Copper Peak was the western hemisphere's biggest ski jump. To this day, it is the only ski flying hill outside of Europe. Interestingly, this site was listed on the National Register of Historic Places in 1973 and designated a Michigan State Historic Site in 1971.

3   My great grandparents made their money from stock market investments. After they passed, they left everything to my aunt Betty Lou, the granddaughter they raised.

4   Roseburg is a small rural town in Oregon that no one had heard of until October 1, 2015, when the Umpqua Community College shooting occurred on campus. Chris Harper-Mercer, a 26-year-old student who was enrolled at the school, fatally shot an assistant professor and eight students in a classroom. Eight others were injured. It's a horrible way to get your hometown recognized. Prior to that, Roseburg was known for an event that literally rocked the town on August 7, 1959, which was probably the most eventful and memorable night in its history. As the story goes, in the early hours of that morning, the Gerretsen Building Supply Company caught fire. Firefighters quickly arrived at the building to assess the situation. Two days earlier, warnings had been issued to the Pacific Powder Company not to leave trucks unattended or park them in congested areas. However, after arranging for his delivery for the following morning, a truck driver for the Pacific Powder Company, George Rutherford, parked his explosives truck in front of the building. The truck was loaded with two tons of dynamite and four and a half tons of nitro-carbo-nitrate. Fortunately, the truck was noticed by two police officers who were on site and able to evacuate the area. It exploded around 1:14 a.m., destroying buildings in an eight block

radius which severely damaged more than 30 blocks, killed fourteen people, and injured 125 more. Damage was estimated at eleven million dollars, and the power company was made to pay $1.2 million in civil damages but was acquitted of wrongdoing. Unfortunately, the two police officers were killed in the blast but were recognized as heroes.

5　As a child, I was fortunate to visit many of the national parks and monuments. By the time I was in my 50s, I had been to every state in the U.S. with the exception of Mississippi and North Carolina.

6　When we did get store-bought clothes, they were from second-hand shops.

7　We didn't recognize it as bullying back then.

8　Molestation as defined in the dictionary is the crime of sexual acts with children up to the age of eighteen, including the touching of private parts, exposure of genitalia, taking pornographic pictures, rape, inducement of sexual acts with the molester or with other children, and variations of these acts by pedophiles.

9　I still avidly follow college and professional football and never get bored.

10　Cloud nine is an idiom that expresses the feeling of being happy.

11　Climax. "Precious and Few." Written by Nims, Walter D. 1971.

12　A whoopee cushion is a practical joke device that makes flatulence humorous.

13　It wasn't until I got much older in life that I learned about the history of maternity homes. These places weren't originally created to hide pregnant teens from prying neighbors and judgmental communities. In fact, in 1883, New York businessman Charles Crittenton founded the Florence Crittenton Mission, which operated the largest number of charity homes in the U.S. that claimed to assist women in need. The homes originally served prostitutes and unwed pregnant women whom the organization aimed to lift up through evangelical efforts. The mission's earliest leaders believed keeping mothers and babies together helped accomplish this goal. In the 1930s and 1940s, as more young women became pregnant out of wedlock, social workers began to classify them as neurotic. By the 1950s, professionals said that the problem of unwed mothers was a psychological one, making them unfit to raise children. By the 1950s, the Florence Crittenton Association of America, the Salvation Army, Catholic Charities, and other organizations operated more than two hundred maternity homes in forty-four states. Altogether, the homes housed around 25,000 young women each year (and turned away thousands more). Young women who stayed in these homes say they were subjected to many layers of secrecy. In some homes, phone calls and visitors were restricted. When the young women left these homes on outings, they had to wear wedding bands provided by staff members. To keep up appearances while they were away, many young women lived a lie to their aunts and uncles and other family members by telling them they were on an extended holiday at a relative's place.

14 Cher. "If I Could Turn Back Time." *Heart of Stone*. Written by Warren, Diane. Produced by Dianne Warren and Guy Roche. 1989.

15 In hindsight, I don't think I was being unreasonable. There were many times when his family went overboard. When we were first married, his entire family would walk into our house, unannounced, because our doors in Oregon were always unlocked. It freaked me out at times and then it got annoying.

16 One day my mother visited and asked, "Why did you put all that weight back on again, Vicky? You know, you have been FAT most of your life and, because you lack discipline, you will always be fat." Her words and tone caused great damage to me.

17 It took years to forgive both myself and Dan, but with the Lord's help, I was able to walk in freedom, not holding against either one of us the fact that we did not stand and fight for our marriage.

18 Foster, David and Thompson, Linda. "Grown-Up Christmas List." Peermusic Publishing, Universal Music Publishing Group, Warner Chappell Music, Inc. 1992.

19 Thomas says he felt like he was under the influence of Satan. He went online to a laboratory supply website and ordered a bottle of Ether, claiming he felt possessed to do so, with the intention of drugging me and making love to me while I was knocked out. He thought this would make things right. He recalls fighting with himself not to use the ether but, the urge was far too strong to resist. In his words, "As I lay there contemplating my actions and inwardly fighting my impulses, I gently placed the washcloth on the pillow next to Vicky's head. A moment later, something spoke to me and asked me what I was doing!? I came to my senses and reached for the washcloth. As I did, Vicky suddenly woke up and asked me what the smell was." To this day, he feels he was not in control of his mind during this period of time between us.

20 Thomas and I were stunned when we learned that Michael's adoptive parents, Dixie and Rick, lived in Colorado. A year earlier, we purchased a home in Colorado where we planned to retire. There were so many coincidences, or were they?

Made in United States
Troutdale, OR
01/21/2024

17028345R00080